DAY-BY-DAY

Reflection Guide for the Engaged and Newly Married

by
John J. Colligan and Kathleen A. Colligan
with
The Broome County Council of Churches

PAULIST PRESS
New York/Mahwah, N.J.

Library of Congress Cataloging-in-Publication Data

Colligan, John.
    Day-by-day: reflection guide for the engaged and newly married / by John J. Colligan and Kathleen A. Colligan with the Broome County Council of Churches.
        p.   cm.
    ISBN 0-8091-3458-6 (pbk.)
    1. Marriage—Religious aspects—Christianity. 2. Marriage—Problems, exercises, etc. I. Colligan, Kathy. II. Broome County Council of Churches. III. Title.
BT706.C64   1994
248.8'44—dc20   93-31032
                                                          CIP

Published by Paulist Press
997 Macarthur Boulevard
Mahwah, NJ 07430

Printed and bound in the
United States of America

Contents

The Day-By-Day Symbol . . .

In the center are your intertwined wedding rings, a sign of your oneness as a couple. Woven through the rings is a dogwood branch. Legend tells us that Jesus was hung on a cross made of dogwood. So the cross of Jesus blesses our Christian marriage. The dogwood is an early spring sign of new life to the world. Your marriage is a sign of new life to the Christian church. When the blossoms fade and fall, the dogwood leaves remain green. When the memories of your courtship fade in time, the beauty of your ongoing love for each other is a witness of Christ's love for his church.

This book is called DAY-BY-DAY as a reminder that your wedding day is only the first day of your Christian marriage, and that your love will grow for each other DAY-BY-DAY.

This symbol was designed and executed by William Mihalko, a Johnson City, N.Y., artist and teacher who has worked extensively with religious symbolism.

A Note from the Authors . . .

We put together this series of observations and exercises to help you go deeper in your relationship in marriage. Sometimes you may find yourselves on a plateau and want to move on, sometimes you'll find yourselves discouraged and in need of hope, sometimes you'll be angry and need to know how to settle your differences.

We believe that when you come to the church for marriage and invite God to be part of your lives together, God blesses that commitment and remains with you throughout your lives together. We hope you'll find some support, encouragement, and at least a few ideas in these pages to help you grow deeper in your love for each other and for God. Be assured God blesses you in all your efforts.

We promise to keep you in our prayers each day.

In the Father's love,

John and Kathy Colligan

A Prayer To Begin . . .

Please pray together the prayer that Jesus taught us, a prayer that is universal to all Christians . . .

> Our Father, who art in heaven,
> hallowed be thy name;
> thy kingdom come;
> thy will be done on earth
> as it is in heaven.
> Give us this day our daily bread;
> and forgive us our trespasses
> as we forgive those
> who trespass against us;
> and lead us not into temptation,
> but deliver us from evil.
>
> Amen.

When You Want To Communicate...

Good communication is the rock on which every strong relationship builds. After we've been married a while, we have a better understanding of how well/poorly we actually communicate. Every couple needs to work on this area of their relationship throughout their marriage.

To communicate deeply and honestly with another person and to be understood and accepted by the other draws the two people into deep intimacy—the intimacy on which a healthy sexual relationship develops and in which the problems of life can be faced in trust and openness.

Communicating with our beloved also teaches us about ourselves as we explore attitudes, opinions, and feelings about Who I Am, and Who You Are, and Who We Are in the World. Although most couples do a lot of this exploring during their courtship, they typically get distracted by the demands of daily living, and fail to appreciate how each of them changes as time goes on. Periodically it is good to review these questions to ensure that we are growing in our awareness of each other.

Called To Be One

As Christians, we are called to be one. Nowhere is that call so demanding or so urgent as in marriage. In our oneness, we'll know complete joy, the joy that Jesus wants for us. In this day of sexual liberation, many couples have no difficulty in establishing a sexual relationship. Some believe that if they have good sex, everything else will take care of itself. But that's not true. Even a good sexual relationship suffers when the general level of communication is poor.

Becoming one as husband and wife certainly includes sexual intimacy but it also includes emotional and spiritual intimacy as well. This can only be done through ongoing verbal and nonverbal communication. Sometimes it is more difficult to be emotionally naked in front of the one we love than it is to be physically naked. Because of our culture, this is especially true for men and women who have never learned how to put their feelings into words and have never experienced a deep level of acceptance.

We All Seek Intimacy

The root meaning of the word "intimacy" is "with fear." Most couples want intimacy with one another but are afraid of it. Much depends on the way they were raised, what their experiences have been like in previous relationships, and their own self-confidence and confidence in their spouse. Sharing yourself deeply with another person and trusting the other person to be open to receiving you always involves an element of risk. We'll have very few intimate relationships in life, and the most intimate one of all is with our spouse. It takes a great deal of trust to become truly intimate. Let's look at a list of reasons why some people find it difficult to communicate.

* * * * *

Below are listed a number of reasons why some people find it difficult to communicate or to talk honestly about their deepest feelings. Go through the list and put a check mark next to every reason why you may find it difficult to share with your spouse on at least some areas of your relationship. (The husband writes his answers in the left hand column, the wife writes her answers on the right.)

HUSBAND WIFE

___	___	I don't know how to communicate.
___	___	I'm afraid it will make you angry.
___	___	I'm not sure I want to get into this.
___	___	Everytime I want to talk, you want to make love.

8

—	—	I have been hurt before by *someone else*. I'm afraid to trust again.
—	—	I've been hurt before by you. I'm afraid to trust again.
—	—	We never have much time to talk without distractions.
—	—	My family never did this.
—	—	None of our friends do this and they seem to be doing all right.
—	—	I don't see myself as a very "deep" person.
—	—	If I tell you everything about me, will you still love me?
—	—	Everytime you say "We need to talk" I think, "Now I'm going to get a lecture."
—	—	We're usually too tired to talk.
—	—	I don't want to start a fight.
—	—	I'm afraid you'll pressure me to change.
—	—	I'm hoping you'll change.
—	—	I'm afraid of a divorce.
—	—	I worry about whether we'll be able to work through our differences if we open up a difficult issue.
—	—	Other _____

Now go back through the list and put a * in your spouse's column next to every reason why you believe your spouse may hold back in sharing with you, at least in some areas.

Identify an area where you would like to know your spouse's feelings more clearly (money, sex, discipline of the children, in-laws, religion, etc.).

_____

Identify an area where you would like to explain your feelings more clearly to your spouse.

_____

Below are some stereotypical comments made about men and women that may or may not be true for the two of you. Go through the list and put a check mark next to each item that you think describes you.

HUSBAND WIFE

___	___	Men are directed outward.
___	___	Women are directed inward.
___	___	A man's self-image focuses on "what I do."
___	___	A woman's self-image focuses on "who I am."
___	___	Men tend to be competitive.
___	___	Women tend to value cooperation.
___	___	Men value independence.
___	___	Women value interdependence.
___	___	Women in talking to women stress their feelings and emphasize relationships.
___	___	Men in talking to men stress external events—what they did, what happened in the world, sports, politics, etc.
___	___	Men don't pay much attention to feelings.
___	___	Women pay a lot of attention to sharing feelings.
___	___	Men tend to be goal-oriented. "We made that decision. Let's move on to something else."
___	___	Women tend to be process-oriented. "I've changed my mind. I want to discuss that decision again."
___	___	Women are more likely to press for good communications than men.

Now go back through the list and put a * in the column for each answer which you believe describes your spouse.

Take a few minutes to share your answers with one another.

Fitting into the Stereotypes

It's often true that women are more likely to press for good verbal communications than men.

Some men enjoy what they can see and experience in their wives: her body, the way she keeps house, the way she loves him and makes love to him, the way she cares for their children.

Most women want their husbands to know and love what cannot be seen: her heart and soul. She wants to love her husband in the same way. She really does want to know what's going on inside of him. Often her husband doesn't know how to put his feelings into words to describe them to her or even to himself.

A man might say, "I talked at work all day. I don't want to talk anymore when I get home. What do we have to talk about anyway? We've already said it all."

A wife might respond, "I need to know the real you, and I need to reveal to you the real me." She believes that what makes her special is not her outer beauty which will eventually fade, but her inner beauty which will grow with time.

Both men and women fear losing themselves and their self-identity by becoming one with the other. The paradox is that we get a clearer picture of who we are as individuals and as a couple when we live in deep intimacy.

Where do you fit in?

Issues or Us

Most couples don't try to keep secrets from one another. Often the reason why people don't discuss a topic is simply because the issue never came up or because they assumed there was no need for discussion. Each may think, "This is the way it was always done in my family and it seemed to work well. I'll just settle this matter the way my mom or dad did." Then they're amazed when their spouse explodes with anger about the decision they've made.

Often the issues that are never discussed become the issues that are most divisive—topics like the division of household chores, attitudes about money, and care and disci-

11

pline of the children. These are the molehills that become mountains. Therefore it's helpful to get as many issues as possible out in the open to make sure we have a clear understanding about what's expected by each of us in our marriage as time and circumstances change in our marriage. Issues don't go away by ignoring them. It's essential that you face your differences as well as your similarities.

Sometimes issues seem bigger than they really are when they're not discussed. By discussing something that seems like a major problem to one of us, we may find that it's not a problem to our spouse at all. Sometimes we believe we're keeping a carefully hidden secret from our spouse and we're afraid to reveal it. Often we may be surprised that our spouse guessed our secret some time ago and still loves us.

Since we tend to adopt the communications style of our family-of-origin and bring it into our own marriage, it's helpful to understand our underlying attitudes about how communications should be handled. Let's go to the next exercise.

* * * * *

Below are a series of statements about your family-of-origin and how they communicated with one another. On the left hand side, under the column *MY FAMILY*, check all those statements that apply to your family-of-origin. If you grew up in more than one home, or were adopted, choose the answers which applied most of the time. On the right hand side, under the column *OUR MARRIAGE*, put a check mark after each statement which applies to your own marriage now.

MY FAMILY		OUR MARRIAGE
___	We never lied to one another.	___
___	We were always able to express feelings honestly.	___
___	We were never too tired or too preoccupied to listen	___
___	We often only partially listened to each other.	___
___	We didn't make snap judgments about the other person.	___
___	We often spoke before the other finished talking.	___

____ We often shouted, pounded a fist, or waved our ____
arms to make a point.
____ We always faced up to our differences. ____
____ We complimented one another often. ____
____ We always looked for the goodness in one ____
another.
____ Criticism was a regular part of life. ____
____ We called each other names. ____
____ We did much good-natured teasing. ____
____ We laughed a great deal and had fun together. ____
____ One member of the family was always tense or ____
defensive.
____ We thought shouting helped us make our point. ____
____ Slamming a door or leaving the house was often ____
part of an argument.
____ Some family members stopped speaking to each ____
other rather than argue.
____ Not speaking to each other is a regular form of ____
punishment in my family.
____ We turned off TV/radio or put down a newspaper ____
to pay attention to each other.
____ We made time to be together just to enjoy one ____
another's company.
____ My parents kept secrets from each other. ____
____ Only weak people cried in front of each other. ____
____ We were openly affectionate with one another. ____
____ My parents often had intimate talks together. ____
____ Forgiveness was a normal part of making up. ____
____ There were no "winners" or "losers" in an ____
argument.
____ When angry, it was permissible to sulk and/or ____
pout.
____ Sulking and pouting helped me get my way. ____
____ Swearing was common in our house. ____
____ We had many secrets from each other. ____
____ Telling the truth was important. ____
____ In an argument people sometimes hit each other. ____
____ I sometimes hit people when I'm angry. ____
____ Mom and dad often spoke the words "I love you" ____
to me and others.

13

___ My parents were openly affectionate with each ___
other.
___ Arguing was not permitted in my family. ___
___ It's easier to show my love than to speak it · ___
directly.
___ I find it difficult to confront issues directly. ___
___ When you ask me what's wrong, I deny anything ___
is wrong.
___ The men in our family refuse to communicate. ___
___ Women in our family manipulate others to get ___
their way.

Of all the statements listed above, which do you regard as the strongest (i.e. most positive) points in your relationship right now? (Put a * next to your strong points.)

Of all the statements listed above, which do you regard as the weakest points in your relationship right now? (Put an X next to the weak points of either you or your spouse.)

What did your family do that you would least like to see repeated in your own marriage?

_____

_____

What did your family do that you would most like to see repeated in your own marriage?

_____

_____

What change can you make right now in order to communicate better with your spouse?

_____

_____

What change would you like your spouse to make in order to help you communicate better as a couple?

_____

I believe we should communicate deeply with each other

_____

(How frequently?) _____

The best time for us to communicate is:

_____

_____

As soon as your spouse is done, share your answers with each other and discuss them in some detail. Take the time you need to fully explain yourself and to truly understand one another.

15

When You Want To Go Deeper in Relationship . . .

In marriage, communication is not an option. We must communicate with one another (both verbally and non-verbally) in order to have true intimacy, and we must communicate our feelings as well as our thoughts and opinions.

Chances are you were already communicating ideas, attitudes, opinions, and beliefs long before you got married. It's what you did when you were getting to know one another. You may have asked these types of questions: "What kind of music do you like?" "What's your family like?" "What kind of family life do you want?" You may have talked about jobs or favorite sports teams or politics.

Hopefully you agree on most of these things. It's important to have shared goals, values, and dreams. But there is even more to learn and understand about each other—your feelings.

A feeling is a pleasurable or painful emotion inside us, which may have been aroused by an exterior event, or by something interior. We can agree/disagree with one another indefinitely about our attitudes and ideas, but feelings are much deeper—part of the core of who we are.

Our feelings are always changing. They arise spontaneously within us. They may not even be rational; we may not know where they came from or how long they'll last. For example, I may get up in the morning feeling irritable. I think, "I got up on the wrong side of the bed." On another day I might feel joyful.

We don't usually know how to explain these feelings even to ourselves. As a married couple, however, we don't have to take out our negative feelings on one another. Even if we feel irritable, we don't have to act that way.

Understanding feelings helps us understand each other

16

on a deeper level. For example, we may both have the same opinion about something, but have very different feelings about it. Let's say you and your spouse both believe: "Every couple should postpone having a family until they have been married at least five years." Underneath your opinions, your feelings may be very different. One of you may have a deep longing for a baby now. Your feelings may be: yearning, loneliness, hunger, and regret about the decision to wait. The other person may feel frightened and anxious about becoming a parent and may feel contentment with the decision.

You can argue about whether or not it's a wise decision to have a baby, but the feelings remain. You can choose to override them, but you should not ignore them. When a couple indefinitely ignores the deep feelings of either one or both of them, they begin to feel misunderstood and often pull away from each other.

It's also true that if we are deeply attentive to what our husband/wife is telling us and absorbing the pain, the loneliness, the discomfort the other is experiencing regardless of the issue, we will have to continue to work on the issue and come to some peaceful, mutually agreeable solution. Feelings are facts and must be considered in all decision making.

We cannot change our spouse, but we can change ourselves. Our reason for deciding to change is based on how our current behavior may cause our spouse discomfort or pain. In other words, we decide to change because we don't want to see our beloved suffer.

We also can't blame one another for our feelings. The feelings simply are. Perhaps they're part of our dream for what our life would be like or part of our expectation of what our marriage should provide. Possibly our dreams haven't come true. Discussion can help to change and mold the future you both want.

Sometimes our spouse says or does something that reminds us of a bad experience in a past relationship. So we lash out at him/her. We need to take responsibility for our own feelings and acknowledge, "It's not your fault I feel this way. Even if you did something that offended me, I am responsible for my reaction."

Everytime you find yourself over-reacting to a situation, stop and ask yourself, "What is there about me that causes me to act this way?" When you've calmed down, you can discuss what triggered the episode and see how together you can avoid future upsets.

Here is a brief exercise to help you sort out thoughts from feelings.

* * * * *

The following two sentences answer the question, "How do you feel right now?" Complete both sentences, using only one word. You may use the same word in both sentences. There is a brief list of feeling words listed below from which you may choose, or you may use your own word that best describes how you feel right now.

How do you feel right now?

I feel _____

I am _____

Feeling Words: happy, sad, bitter, bored, afraid, eager, nervous, anxious, hurt, sincere, delighted, excited, irritable, angry, joyful, tired, etc.

Describe your feeling. (How strong is it? When have you felt this way before?)

_____

_____

Now complete these two sentences to describe your opinion about something.

I think _____

I feel that _____

Share your responses with your spouse for a few minutes.

18

Whenever we can substitute the words "I am" for "I feel" and still have a meaningful sentence, we have probably described a feeling. For example, "I feel happy" and "I am happy" both make sense. Note how often people use the sentence, "I feel that...." They are not describing a feeling; it's a judgment, opinion, or idea.

Losing That "Loving Feeling"

One thought that terrifies most couples is what to do when they've "lost that loving feeling." Love is much more than a single feeling. There are many feelings that constitute love: warmth, closeness, caring, compassion, understanding, etc.

In every marriage there are times when we feel nothing at all toward one another—in which case we feel indifferent. Sometimes we have negative feelings about each other—in which case we feel hurt, angry, frustrated, annoyed, etc. Some days we may wonder why we got married at all—which means we feel fearful or doubtful about our decision to marry this person.

When you don't feel "in love," try to identify what's going on. Maybe it's only a passing thing. We're not going to feel "up" every day, but that doesn't mean love has ended. It may mean we have to spend more time together, work on our relationship, pray for passion in our marriage, and, if necessary, get some counseling.

Even if we don't feel loving, we can still act in a loving way. Love is a decision. We can decide to love each other every day of our lives.

Listening vs. Hearing

We also need to understand the difference between listening and hearing. Hearing focuses on self, making sure I get accurate information. A tape recorder is a perfect hearer.

19

Listening focuses on the other person. Here are some ways to be a better listener to your spouse:

1. Find a quiet spot away from all other distractions (radio, TV, children, newspaper, etc.).
2. Look into each other's eyes.
3. Hold hands.
4 Read nonverbal as well as verbal communication, i.e. tears forming in the eyes, tension in the face, wringing of hands, etc.
5. Give positive feedback. "What I hear you saying is..." "Is that correct?"
6. Restate the case if necessary.
7. Don't listen with your motor running, waiting your turn so you can say what you have to say.
8. Do not tell the other person not to feel that way. Do try to take on that feeling.

Most people say they don't communicate because they are too busy, but communicating doesn't need to take a lot of time. Let's do a Listening Exercise to demonstrate how well two people can communicate in just five minutes time.

Listening Exercise

1. Choose a topic about which you urgently wish to communicate with your spouse (opinions about God, sex, death, money, in-laws, a strong belief or opinion you have, etc.).
2. One of you will be the listener and one of you will be the speaker. Choose right now which of you will go first. That person is the speaker.
3. The speaker talks for one minute to the listener about the topic he/she has chosen, expressing not only beliefs and opinions but feelings as well.
4. The listener listens as intently as possible (holding hands, looking into the speaker's eyes, reading the body language of the speaker, looking for clues behind all that is being said).
5. After one minute, the speaker stops and the listener will feed back what he/she heard the speaker say. The listener

has one minute to respond without being interrupted. Report back what you saw and read into the speaker's words by the body language as well as by the spoken words.

6. After one minute, the listener stops and gives the speaker thirty seconds to respond and to correct the listener if necessary.

7. Then switch roles—the speaker will become the listener and the listener will become the speaker—and repeat the exercise.

When You're Disappointed in One Another . . .

From time to time in every relationship we are bound to be disappointed by the behavior of one another. In the intimacy of marriage, we experience our own sinfulness and the sinfulness of our beloved most closely. And because we expect so much of ourselves and one another in marriage, we are also most vulnerable to the hurt that comes from sin.

In the first letter of John in scripture, we are reminded that we are all sinners: "If we say that we have no sin, we deceive ourselves, and the truth is not in us. If we confess our sins, he who is faithful and just will forgive us our sins and cleanse us from all unrighteousness. If we say that we have not sinned, we make him a liar, and his word is not in us" (1 Jn 1:8-10).

Sometimes, even when we are trying to be at our best and sincerely live for the sake of the other, we may hurt our spouse because that person was expecting something more from us. At such times we find ourselves making judgments about one another. The wonderful, kind, thoughtful, sensitive person you thought you married doesn't behave that way all the time. You may decide you have married an insensitive, inconsiderate, selfish person, whose major goal is to disrupt your plans and ruin your life.

At this point some couples panic and decide to run—either by separating and divorcing—or, less dramatically, but still powerfully, by withdrawing from one another—becoming less close, less trusting, and less caring. The inner response to the disappointment is, "If I can't count on you, then I'll take care of myself." Some use their sexual relationship as a weapon to get even—avoiding intercourse for long periods of time—and that only drives them further apart.

Don't Panic

Before deciding on any course of action, take time to reflect on your own life and your lives together. Jesus tells us again and again not to judge one another. Are you judging your spouse harshly—attributing to that person harsh motives that really aren't there?

Are you communicating clearly your needs and expectations? Some people never learned how to communicate well. As children, their parents may have instinctively responded to their needs. Or sometimes we think we're communicating clearly, and we're not communicating at all. Sometimes we have the belief, "If you really loved me, I wouldn't have to tell you what I want or need." That's ridiculous.

* * * * *

When things go wrong and we are disappointed, we often blame one another. We forget that everyone makes mistakes from time to time. Most of us do dumb things that we wish we hadn't done. What are some of the things that have happened or are likely to happen in your relationship?

Put a check mark next to those items which you are likely to do. The husband writes his answers in the Husband Column. The wife writes her answers in the Wife Column. Then go back through the list and put a * next to the those things you think your spouse is likely to do. The space marked Other is to add any items that upset either of you.

HUSBAND WIFE

HUSBAND	WIFE	
___	___	Leave car with empty gas tank.
___	___	The lights get left on in an empty room.
___	___	The heat doesn't get turned down at night.
___	___	The paycheck is misplaced.
___	___	The checking account is overdrawn.
___	___	The milk is spilled.
___	___	One of us forgets to buy coffee/milk, etc.
___	___	Something is broken and you haven't fixed it yet.

NOW	BEGIN	
___	___	One of us was supposed to be some- where and wasn't there.
___	___	The car was dented.
___	___	The rent/mortgage wasn't paid on time.
___	___	We forgot to respond to an invitation.
___	___	A job that got started wasn't finished.
___	___	One of us is chronically late.
___	___	I counted on you to do something, and you didn't.
___	___	Messages aren't passed on accurately.
___	___	Other _____

When both of you have finished writing your responses, exchange them and talk about how you react with each other when these situations arise. Discuss how it affects the closeness of your relationship. Talk for at least fifteen minutes.

Some Guidelines

The last thing a Christian marriage needs is for two people to start blaming one another when things go wrong. Here are a few simple guidelines to help you through a disappointing experience. In Exercise Two consider how many of these guidelines you are already practicing and which ones you'd like to start practicing.

* * * * *

Put a check mark in the column marked NOW for those items which describe your current behavior. Put a * in the column marked BEGIN for those items which you want to start practicing in your marriage.

NOW BEGIN
___	___	1. Acknowledge that there is a problem. (We don't seem to be communicating very well in this area.)
___	___	2. Assume the goodness of the other person. (He intended to be on time. She didn't dent the car on purpose.)

| | | 3. | Agree on a mutual long-term goal. (We both want to have a happy marriage with love and trust between us.) |

___ ___ 3. Agree on a mutual long-term goal. (We both want to have a happy marriage with love and trust between us.)

___ ___ 4. Talk about how you can mutually reach that goal. (Only one of us should use the checkbook. "I will leave written reminders when I want you to pick up something from the store." "I will write down messages for you.")

___ ___ 5. Make a decision not to blame one another when something bad does happen. (No name-calling. No ridicule or sarcasm. No criticism. "I know I can tell you about anything that has happened and you won't insult or attack me.")

___ ___ 6. Decide how you can together solve the current problem. (If the milk is spilled, we can clean it up together. If the car is dented, we can celebrate that our spouse is unhurt and together make arrangements for the car's repair.)

___ ___ 7. Don't punish each other. (Recognize that you are both adults and don't need to be treated like children.)

We Choose To Live as Victims, Or We Take Charge of Our Lives

In life, things don't always turn out as we have planned. It's also true that some people are more clumsy, more forgetful or poorer at handling money than others. As a married couple, however, we can choose our response to life's situations, regardless of how the difficulty arose. We can work together to overcome the problem and grow in confidence in ourselves and one another or we can stand back and ridicule the other person and demand that he/she conform to our standards.

It's difficult to build a close, intimate relationship with someone who sees himself/herself as superior to the other. Neither of us married a mother or father figure. We married an equal, a person we admired and respected. We owe it to ourselves to maintain that love and respect throughout our lives. Our home should be a refuge where we can always be ourselves.

Criticism

Most of us have been taught from our earliest days that the only way we can get others to change their behavior is by criticizing them. As children we sang the little song, "Sticks and stones will break my bones, but words will never hurt me." But as we reflect on our lives we realize that most of us spend a large part of our adult years trying to repair the damage done to our self-image by the criticism we received as we were growing up. Critical words do hurt us. They damage our spirit and cause us to be less close in relationship with the one who is the critic.

As we get more sophisticated, we call it "constructive criticism." If someone says, "I'm going to tell you something for your own good," run for your life.

If we want to grow closer to each other in our marriage we must eliminate criticism from our daily lives. If we don't try to do this, we will find our marriage gradually growing colder and colder. Hurting each other with our tongues will become so common that we will habitually react in a critical way.

One sixty-five year old wife told of the pain in her daily life because her husband was so critical. One day she accidentally drove their car into the mailbox, knocked it over, and dented the car. She was very frightened and trembling. As her husband ran out of the house, she expected he was coming to help her. Instead he rushed right past her and immediately surveyed the damage to the car and mailbox. Then he swore at her and told her how stupid she was to do such a thing. Why didn't she look where she was going? That's his form of constructive criticism. Her response to this daily criticism was that after forty-two years of marriage, she was ready to leave him. She commented, "I don't think he sees me as human anymore."

26

Criticism or Correction?

There is an important distinction to be made between criticism and correction. Criticism always attacks and insults the person. Correction addresses only the desired change in behavior.

Consider the following situation handled by criticism one time and by correction another time. Sally is thirteen years old, and her bedroom is a mess in desperate need of cleaning. A critical mom might say: "Sally, your room is filthy. You live like a pig. Not only are you a dirty, sloppy girl, but you're lazy besides. You never do anything around this house. You're no good, you never were any good, you'll never be any good." Sally and her mom just grow farther apart from each other and the room stays dirty.

Addressing the same problem with correction in mind, her mom might say, "Sally, I've asked you a number of times to clean your room. This Saturday I'll work with you as long as it takes to get it cleaned up. If you won't do this, you won't be permitted to go to the party at your friend's house." The room may or may not be clean, but at least mother and daughter have not driven a wedge between them.

As adults, we also need to discuss where a change in behavior is needed. We recommend that it be done at a time when you are both well-rested and at peace with each other. Talk about how you feel when a certain negative behavior occurs. Talk without blaming or criticizing. Ask your spouse what changes are possible. Inquire how you can help your spouse change.

For example, "When you use a harsh tone of voice with me, I hurt inside. I find myself getting very defensive and deeply offended. Then I know I pull away from you. I don't want to be anywhere around you. Is there another way we can handle this situation?" Discuss changes you can both make to bring about a better atmosphere in your home. Begin by agreeing to eliminate criticism from your marriage and you will have taken a major step in reducing tension, hurt and disappointment in one another.

When You're Having an Argument . . .

Some couples say they never argue. Others seem to be arguing all the time. Having an honest disagreement in a relationship is not a bad thing and is bound to happen from time to time, especially when two people are living in the deep intimacy of a lifelong marriage. In fact, not arguing can be a negative sign—a sign of lack of trust or confidence in the relationship or perhaps of fear about what may happen if you do differ on the issues between you.

It's important to remember that in marriage the deep-seated issues do not go away. We may both be able to ignore them for a long time, but sooner or later we'll have to face up to them—or else live increasingly separate lives. On the other hand, facing up to the issues as they arise helps us to deal with them one at a time, while they are still relatively minor. As we handle these issues, we grow in our confidence and trust, knowing that our relationship can withstand all things—even the storms of life.

Since much of our response to an argument is buried within us, it's helpful to understand how we came to form our attitudes about handling differences of opinion. We'll begin by looking at our families of origin.

* * * * *

A. In our family, when my parents argued or there was a difference of opinion, they did the following things. (In the first column check those items that best describe your mother's behavior. In the second column check those items that best describe your father's behavior. If you were raised in a single parent family, check those items that best describe how that parent handled family fights.)

MY   MY
MOM DAD

___ ___ Avoided an argument at all costs.
___ ___ Would administer the "silent treatment".
___ ___ Would become cold and indifferent. (For how
          long? _____)
___ ___ Would most likely confront the issues.
___ ___ Would often scream or shout.
___ ___ Would call the other person names.
___ ___ Would slam doors, pots and pans, etc.
___ ___ Would throw things.
___ ___ Would leave the house.
___ ___ Would physically attack the other person.
___ ___ Would sit down to discuss the issues between
          them.
___ ___ Would build up to a fight for days or weeks at
          a time.
___ ___ Would refuse to forgive the other person.
___ ___ Would always try to come out a "winner."
___ ___ Would continue to bring up an argument long
          after it was over.
___ ___ Reconciled their differences as soon as
          possible.
___ ___ Would write letters explaining his/her
          position.
___ ___ Other_____

Who was most likely to start an argument?

_____

_____

Who was most likely to bring it to a conclusion or seek reconciliation first?

_____

_____

Go through the list above and put a * next to those items that best describe your behavior today with your spouse.

B. As a child, what was your response to hearing your parents argue (or your single parent and any significant person in his/her life?)

___ I was afraid. ___ I cried. ___ I hid.
___ I never remember an argument. ___ I had no reaction.
___ I vowed never to behave like that.
___ I thought they handled it well.
___ I never paid any attention to them.
___ I left the house or made myself scarce.
___ I decided I would never argue.
___ I decided all people behaved that way when angry.
___ I took sides. ___ I became the mediator.
___ I'm still involved in my parent's (parents') arguments.
___ Other _____

C. Go through the list below and check those issues on which your parents were most likely to disagree. Then go back through the list and check the issues on which you and your spouse disagree.

MY PARENTS	US	
___	___	Money
___	___	Sex
___	___	In-laws
___	___	Where we'll live
___	___	Division of household chores
___	___	Religious practices
___	___	Discipline of the children
___	___	How we'll spend our leisure time
___	___	How we're treating one another
___	___	Care of health
___	___	Friends
___	___	Habits
___	___	Other _____

D. What are the strongest reasons that prevent you from confronting an issue between you and your spouse?

___ Fear of losing my spouse's love.
___ Fear of divorce.
___ Fear of losing my spouse's respect.
___ Negative memories from my childhood.
___ Fear of "losing" the argument.
___ Fear that my spouse will withhold sex.
___ Sense of futility. We argue about the same things all the time.
___ My spouse won't face up to the issues.
___ I avoid facing up to the issues.
___ Fear of violence (either my own or my spouse's).
___ Fear of offending my spouse.
___ I prefer peace at any price.
___ Other _____

After you have both finished writing your responses, share them with each other and spend at least fifteen minutes discussing how these behaviors affect your marriage relationship.

How To Argue Constructively

Having an argument or strong disagreement in a marriage is never a pleasant experience. However, there are some things to keep in mind that can help to make even our disagreements a positive growth experience for both of us.

1. *Face up to the issues*. It's important to clear the air and not allow hurt to come between you.
2. *Set aside time to have your argument*. Don't start a fight on your way out to work. Acknowledge that you have a difference of opinion and set a time when you can get together without interruptions to discuss the issue.
3. If you find yourself really furious, *take the time to calm down first*. Admit that you are deeply angry and decide when you will be calm enough to talk without attacking the other person (preferably within the next forty-eight hours).

31

4. *Focus on the issue.* Make sure the issue you're arguing about is the real issue. (Often the real issue is, "I don't think you love me anymore, or you wouldn't behave this way.")

5. *Work only on one issue at a time.* Don't bring up past history. Don't make general statements like, "You *always* do this" or "You *never* do that."

6. *Work only on the current issue.* Your spouse can account for his/her behavior during the past few days. It's not possible to defend the past ten years.

7. *Don't threaten divorce.* A marriage is for a lifetime. Sometimes idle threats become harsh realities.

8. *Don't call in others:* your children, your mom or dad, or your best friend. Do call a counselor for input and clarification if you continue to have differences that cannot be resolved.

9. *Sit down together* to face the issue and argue. *Look at each other. Listen to each other. Hold hands.* This is a difficult time for both of you.

10. *Don't call each other names,* insult or attack one another. *Don't walk out, throw things, slam doors or otherwise physically threaten or abuse* the other person. Such antics make for great television drama but they destroy relationships.

11. *Don't be hypersensitive* and cry over the least thing or refuse to talk. Don't take offense at everything that's said.

12. Listen to what your spouse is telling you about your relationship with one another. Often we are learning about our own sinfulness and shortcomings. It's hard to hear this. *Acknowledge where you are wrong and make plans to change your behavior* in the future.

13. *Finish the fight.* Don't let it drag on for days or weeks. St. Paul tells us, "Do not let the sun go down on your anger, and do not make room for the devil" (Eph 4:26-27).

14. Remember that you are probably both right—at least to some extent. That's why you're arguing. *Acknowledge that on some issues you may have to agree to disagree* until you can get more input into the situation. Decide how you're both going to try to work toward a resolution.

15. *Forgive one another* for anything that has been said or done that has hurt the other.
16. *Hold each other* and remember that you are more important than any issues that divide you.
17. *Say a prayer together,* thanking God for bringing this person into your life, and asking God to be with you in the future as you work together to live in love.

Remember that God is, and always has been, with you in your marriage. You came to the church to ask God to bless your marriage. By facing a difficult situation together, you have placed your trust in God and the goodness of your spouse. You have lived by God's law of love. You have been patient and kind. You have not been harsh or judgmental. You have been forgiving and you have asked forgiveness. You have grown in Christian maturity and faith.

When the Hurt Lingers On...

In every intimate human relationship there are bound to be hurt feelings and misunderstandings in spite of our best efforts to love one another and place each other first. It often surprises us when hurt enters our relationship—especially if we really didn't intend to offend each other in the first place. But suddenly there's a blow-up between us or just a silent rift that gradually deepens. Maybe we aren't even aware of it until a few days or months go by and we look back and realize, "We're not having fun together anymore." Or we begin to wonder, "Whatever happened to the closeness we once had?"

Identifying the Hurt

Hurt comes from many places and not always from each other. Nevertheless, even if we've been hurt by something outside our relationship, we often take it out on each other. Below are a few areas where hurt might occur.

* * * * *

Go through the list and check any area(s) where you may have been hurt now or in the past. If you are currently hurting, then put a * next to the description that best describes what happened. Use this as a starting point for self-understanding as well as shared discussion.

___ I expected you to do something or respond in a certain way and you didn't.

___ I was hoping you would listen to me and take my part, and that didn't happen.

___ Sometimes you seem more interested in others than in me.

___ I was looking forward to a special kind of relation-
ship, and I fear it's not going to happen between us.
___ I have some difficult times at work.
___ The children/the baby/our parents can really get to
me.
___ I am disappointed in myself at times.
___ I have been hurt in the past by family, friends,
ex-spouse, etc. A present reminder of a past hurt can
get me going.
___ Sometimes I'm angry with God, and that affects me.

Another place to identify hurt is to ask yourself:

1. Where am I frustrated? _____

_____

2. Where have I failed? _____

_____

3. Where am I most angry? _____

_____

4. Whom am I most likely to criticize? _____

_____

How does this affect our relationship?_____

_____

Acknowledging the Hurt

Sometimes we don't like to admit we've been hurt, and
we usually don't like to admit that we take our hurt out on
others. Yet all of us do, even if only in subtle ways, by becom-

ing preoccupied and distant. The nature of marriage is so intimate and personal that if one of us is hurt, the other is bound to be affected also. That's why communication is so important—as well as reconciliation.

Jesus tells us in the gospel of Luke: "Love your enemies, do good to those who hate you, bless those who curse you, pray for those who abuse you. If anyone strikes you on the cheek, offer the other also; and from anyone who takes away your coat do not withhold even your shirt. Give to everyone who begs from you; and if anyone takes away your goods, do not ask for them again. Do to others as you would have them do to you" (Lk 6:27-31).

Jesus is not asking us to live in abusive relationships. Where serious abuse is taking place, counseling is certainly indicated. However for those in normal, healthy relationships where hurt has become part of our lives, we need to seriously consider Jesus' words.

The enemies we most need to forgive usually do not live in a foreign country. Our enemies are the people we love whom we expect to love and accept us. When they cannot do this or will not do this, it hurts. No one can hurt us like our own family members because we expect so much of them.

When hurt occurs, we need to take action in the same way Jesus taught us. We *must* forgive one another. That's the only way we'll find inner peace or bring true peace to our home. We are often reminded in scripture that as we forgive, we will be forgiven. Forgiveness is not an option for a Christian.

Asking for forgiveness and granting it should be a normal part of every marriage relationship. Whenever one of us has been hurt, we can be sure that both of us are hurt because our relationship is a mutual, living entity. Here's a formula for forgiveness that really works—and it's a great way to bring reconciliation between you.

Forgiving One Another

1. Acknowledge that a hurt has taken place in your relationship.
2. The first person says to the second: *"I am sorry for..."*

(whatever the hurt might have been: ...not listening to you, ...withholding my love from you, ...yelling at you, etc.). *"Will you forgive me?"*

3. The second person *always* answers: *"Yes. I forgive you."* (It is very difficult to ask for forgiveness. Therefore, when one person asks, we must grant it and work out the problem later when we're at peace with one another.)

4. Since both persons are hurt, the second person says, *"I'm sorry, too, for..."* (mention the offense: ...being self-righteous and indignant, ...being superior and condescending, ...walking away from you when you needed me, etc.). "Will you forgive me?"

5. The first person responds, *"Yes. I forgive you."*

6. Then both persons *hug each other*. (Sometimes this hug is the only thing that makes the hurt go away. It reminds us of how important we are to one another.)

This formula for forgiveness is not to be used to indefinitely shelve the issues. On the contrary, it can defuse a tense and difficult situation so we can begin to deal with the issues.

In the parable of the prodigal son (Lk 15:11-32), the son returns to the father and asks to be taken in. The father, who is often seen as a symbol of God, not only forgives the son but also embraces him and restores him to a place of honor in the family. In the same way, married couples bring God's love alive to each other as we continually reconcile and forgive the big and little hurts in our lives.

[For additional discussion about hurt and forgiveness, especially from hurts occurring outside marriage, see *The Healing Power of Love* by John and Kathleen Colligan, Paulist Press, 1988.]

When You Want To Talk About Sex/Sexuality . . .

Part A: What Did I Learn About Sex from Mom and Dad?

Throughout history the gift of sexuality has often been misused and misunderstood. Sometimes it hasn't been seen as a gift at all, but as a burden we must tolerate.

In many families sexuality has been treated as something dirty or shameful. The domestic issues of today include abuse and incest. It can be a painful experience to discuss this with your spouse. If you have been abused and have not had counseling, you may want to talk to your pastor about getting help.

Many treat sexuality strictly as an activity—something to do on a date—or as a commodity—a way to sell yourself or to sell something to others. In our culture sexuality is equated with lust or pornography, and it has distorted our understanding of the gift of sexuality.

It's difficult to rid ourselves of all the misinformation, suggestive advertising, bad teaching, bad experiences and previous history we share in this area. Psychologists tell us that ninety percent of our sexual stimulation comes from our brain, so it is essential that we look at how we've been influenced by the society in which we live.

Our attitudes shape our behavior. Therefore, it's important to understand the attitudes you each bring with you to your relationship. The following exercise will help you in this important area.

* * * * *

How old were you when you got your first information about sex/sexuality?

38

_____

_____

What did you learn?

_____

_____

When did you get your first information about sexual intercourse?

_____

_____

What were you told?

_____

_____

Imagine that you're a child again and sitting at the family dinner table with everyone in your family present (brothers, sisters, grandparents, parents, etc.). You ask a question about sex. How would your family react? (Be specific about each member of your family. How would _each_ react?)

NAME   REACTION

_____   _____

_____   _____

_____   _____

_____   _____

_____   _____

What does this tell you about your family's attitudes about sex and sexuality?

_____

_____

Now recall your friends talking about sex/sexuality—especially as you became a young adult. What did they tell you about men, women, relationships, marriage?

_____

_____

What was their primary source of information?

_____

_____

How would you like your own children to learn about sex and sexuality?

_____

_____

Why?

_____

_____

When it comes to discussing sex and sexuality, which of the following statements would best describe you? (You may check more than one statement.)

___ I am very comfortable discussing sex and sexuality with others.

___ I am comfortable discussing sex and sexuality with my husband/wife.

___ I am eager to learn all I can.

___ I have reverence and awe for the gift of sexuality.

___ Sex is something private which good people don't discuss.

___ I am eager to explore this whole area more fully.

___ I don't want to change my attitudes or behavior.

___ I feel pressured by the whole issue.

___ I don't believe there's anything for me to learn.

___ I'd rather not talk about it.

___ I know I will never change.

___ I feel guilty and/or threatened.

___ This is a very difficult area for me to talk about.

___ Other _____

Why? _____

When I hear the word "sex," I think of ... (Check all that apply.)

___ Tenderness	___ Trust	___ Terror
___ Affection	___ Babies	___ Lust
___ Fear	___ Joy	___ Disgust
___ Sleep	___ Birth control	___ Cuddling
___ New techniques	___ Playfulness	___ Orgasm
___ Belonging	___ Faithfulness	___ Wonder
___ Commitment	___ Being used	___ God
___ Giving myself to you	___ Bad memories	___ Romance
___ Satisfaction	___ Dirty jokes	___ Marriage
___ Communication	___ Pornography	___ Reverence

Discuss each set of answers with your spouse. Focus not only on the answers, but on why your spouse answered in that way. Really reach for understanding and acceptance.

***   ***   ***   ***

What Is God's Vision for Us?

The Song of Solomon (8:6-7) celebrates the passion to which we are called to one another in marriage.

> Set me as a seal upon your heart,
>   as a seal upon your arm;
> for love is strong as death,
>   passion fierce as the grave.
> Its flashes are flashes of fire,
>   a raging flame.
> Many waters cannot quench love,
>   neither can floods drown it.
> If one offered for love
>   all the wealth of his house,
>   it would be utterly scorned.

Too often in life we settle for so much less than God has in mind for us. The Christian marriage relationship is to be passionate and sexual. Too often we see couples live more like a good brother and sister rather than passionate lovers. We call it "settling down." Think about it for a moment. If your brother or sister were to come to live with you, what would you expect of that relationship? Most likely you would want them to be thoughtful and considerate, to help out around the house, to let you know if they can't be home on time or be available for dinner, and to occasionally go out with you to dinner, the movies or some other event. That's a good relationship, but it's not Christian marriage. By its very nature, Christian marriage is both sexual and passionate. It is focused intensely on the other. It should include all of the things listed above, but it includes so much more—our passionate desire for one another that grows over time, not diminishes.

This doesn't mean we'll be having sex all the time. It does mean that we will continually choose to focus on the goodness and beauty of the other person, that we will praise and affirm the other, that we will be grateful to God for the gift of one another and that we will desire one another passionately. Our love is to grow more intense over the years.

We have one more exercise.

* * * * *

In the home where I grew up, the sexual atmosphere was generally (check all that apply):

___	Nonexistent	___	Affectionate
___	Open and loving	___	Open but not loving
___	Trusting	___	Caring
___	Healthy	___	Unhealthy
___	Closed	___	Tense
___	Abusive	___	Free and easy
___	Other _____		

The sexual atmosphere I would like to have between us in our home is

_____

_____

Why?_____

Part B: Who Makes the Rules in Our House?

When our sexual relationship is no more than an activity—something we do with one another to feel good or satisfy ourselves—it loses its focus and can become boring and repetitious.

We might refer to our sexual relationship as "it"—and we'll either do "it" or fail to do "it" depending on our mood, our degree of tiredness, or the other distractions in our life. We speak of our "sex life" as though it were something apart from our regular life.

We set up unwritten rules for how we'll live out our "sex life." Here are some typical rules.

1. We'll never do "it" with the lights on.

43

2. We'll only do "it" in the bedroom.
3. We'll never do "it" when the children are up.
4. We'll never do "it" when visiting or when others are visiting us.
5. We won't do "it" after the bed has been made.
6. We'll only do "it" after we've showered.
7. We'll only do "it" at bedtime—if we're both in the mood.

We make up rules to control the behavior of our spouse. The rules come from fear. Often, but not always, the rule-maker is the wife. She makes the rules because she believes her husband is irresponsible or insensitive to her needs. She may also believe her husband is always satisfied in sex and always ready for sex—which may not be the case. The rules convey the message, "I find you very resistible. You aren't that necessary in my life." Irresponsibility says, "I want you to satisfy *my* needs; I'm not really interested in yours." "I'm not listening to you."

Both sentiments convey an attitude of superiority and/or indifference toward the other. "If only you were more like me, things would be better." In order to break the impasse, husband and wife must communicate often about all aspects of their sexual relationship—both verbally and nonverbally.

When our sexual relationship is no more than an activity, it can become routine. We make love on schedule—every Tuesday and Saturday night. We read the public opinion polls and compare ourselves to other couples our age, with our education, and in our socio-economic bracket, to see how often others are doing "it." We put pressure on each other and focus on method and technique. We may become more competent but are less passionate.

We lose our sense of wonder about each other. Sexual intercourse is no longer a wonderful gift from God that we build on all day long. Instead, it's what we do when we go to bed at night, when we're totally exhausted and neither of us wants to put much effort into it.

When sex is treated as activity, we're robbing ourselves of all the joy and intimacy God wants us to share in marriage. Making love is *NOT something we do,* it's *who we are* to one another. Just as we can decide to make love, we can decide to work at being in love twenty-four hours a day. That calls for responsibility, sensitivity and attentiveness on both parts. When pornography is involved in either of our lives, sex and sexuality are degraded for both of us. Our spouse becomes no more than a body to use for our satisfaction. Pornography always distorts our sexuality.

The following exercise may help you go deeper in understanding one another. Please don't pressure each other; just listen and try to understand. Be honest and compassionate with each other.

* * * * *

Go through the statements below and check those that *most frequently* describe your sexual relationship with one another.

Sex for us now is:
____   An exciting and meaningful experience.
____   Fitted into the day like working and cleaning.
____   An expression of physical need.
____   A burden to me.
____   A way to continue to grow closer.
____   Something I do because it's expected of me.
____   A way for one of us to dominate the other.
____   A celebration when we're feeling romantic
____   A release of tension and pressures
____   Something we take for granted.
____   Filled with "rules"
____   Other _____

When do we talk with each other about sex and sexuality? (Check all that apply.)
____   We seldom or never talk about it.
____   When a problem arises.
____   When I'm in a romantic mood.
____   When you're in a romantic mood.
____   When we feel trusting with one another.
____   When we want to change one another.
____   When we want to learn more about each other.
____   When we are frustrated with each other.

45

___ When we're arguing and want to hurt each other.
___ Other _____

What holds me back from talking more with you about our sexual relationship?
___ Fear of offending you.   ___ Don't want to argue.
___ Fear of turning you on.   ___ We have no time to talk.
___ It's not proper to talk about it.
___ We're usually too tired to talk.
___ We're too busy to talk.
___ I'm embarrassed to talk about it.
___ I don't want to rock the boat.
___ I figure we can work it all out later.
___ We discuss sex and sexuality regularly.
___ We have achieved perfect understanding and acceptance of one another's views.
___ I don't want to be criticized.
___ I sense you don't want to talk about it.
___ I'm afraid you'll ask me to change.
___ I'm uncomfortable with some of your attitudes but don't want to hurt you by bringing them up.
___ I don't see the need to talk.
___ I don't want you to know how ignorant I am about it.
___ Other _____

Exchange your answers with your spouse and go over them, one section at a time. Be sure to listen attentively to one another. Ask questions. Find out why your spouse answered as he/she did. Make sure you really understand one another.

Who's in Control?

In every marriage there is often an unspoken desire for control, and one partner often takes control of the sexual relationship. We generally believe this to be the person who initiates sex—the one who says, either verbally or nonverbally, "Let's make love tonight." The person who is really in control however, is the one who has the power to say, "Yes, we will," or "No, we won't."

46

In every marriage, one person also has control of how well and how frequently the couple will communicate with one another—how often they'll have intimate conversation. We may believe that the one who has this power is the one who says, "We've got to talk," or "I wish you'd just listen to me." But the one who has real power over communications is the one who says, "Yes, we will talk," or "No, I won't."

In most (but not all) marriages, it is the woman who is in control of the sexual relationship and the man who is in control of their conversation. God invites us to enter into a relationship defined by mutuality, where we each give up power over the other, where we are mutually submissive to one another.

In every marriage there is deep need for both good verbal communication and a strong sexual relationship. Without both, there is a sense of resentment on the part of one or the other, a feeling of being cheated of something. When a wife lets her husband know she is not interested in him sexually (either by telling him or by simply avoiding him), she may simply be stating, "I don't feel like *it*," or "I'm too tired to do *it*." But what he hears is, "I'm not interested in *you* tonight. I don't want *you*." He takes it as a personal rejection of him.

When a husband tells his wife he's not interested in talking with her, he may simply be saying, "I'm tired. I've worked hard all day and I just want to be left alone." But what she hears is, "I'm not interested in *you* or how you feel. I don't care about *you*." She takes it as personal rejection of her.

The key to a successful marriage is good communications, both verbally and nonverbally. We are called to give up our focus on self in marriage and to focus on one another and our relationship. Sometimes we will make love when one of us doesn't feel like it, and we'll have intimate talks when one of us would rather be doing something else. Then we can ask God to send us the grace we need to be caring and attentive at that moment.

When we simply are too tired, too sick or too distracted to focus on one another either in conversation or in lovemaking, then we should explain with gentleness and love— and set a time when we will make love or talk. We can make a definite date for sometime within the next twenty-four hours. In this way our beloved will know that he/she is still deeply loved and that it's only with regret that we have to postpone our time together. Sexual intercourse does not have to be spontaneous in order to be exciting and fulfilling.

Sexual intercourse is the most powerful form of nonverbal communication between a husband and wife. When a man and woman make love, a bond forms between them—a bond that turns them toward one another rather than away. They tend to be more attentive, listen better, be more affectionate and gentle with each other.

Even two strong independent people are more likely to give up some of that independence and allow the other person to influence them. Making love tends to "gentle us down." The passionate love of a man and woman in Christian marriage is so much more than duty, responsibility, or activity. It is a relationship that is total, giving, creative, committed, enthusiastic, and hopeful.

* * * * *

Use the next few exercises to help you understand one another more.

How do we say "No" to one another in sexual intercourse? (Check all those that apply.)

___	Verbal "No!"	___	"Not again" look
___	"I'm tired."	___	Not bathing
___	"Not now."	___	"Well...if you really want to."
___	"Again?"	___	Being a martyr
___	Going to sleep	___	"Wake me when it's over."
___	Clothing we wear	___	Uninvolvement all day long
___	Reading or TV	___	"I don't feel well."

Who assumes the following responsibilities in our sexual relationship? (Write the initials of either you or your spouse in the appropriate space. If neither of you assume the responsibility, leave the space blank.)

___ How often we'll have sex.
___ When and where we'll have sex.
___ What we will/won't do in sex.
___ Family planning.

___ Quality of our sexual relationship.
___ Taking care of our children physically and emotionally.
___ Initiating sex most of the time.
___ Satisfying my spouse.
___ Creating atmosphere of love all day long.
___ Listening intently to the other in conversation.
___ Making opportunities for quiet time together.

What is our biggest challenge in our sexual relationship now? (Check all that apply.)

___ Tiredness	___ Indifference
___ Boredom	___ Differing ideas
___ Too routine	___ Lack of time together
___ Child/children	___ Lack of romance
___ Parents/in-laws	___ Lack of money
___ Different bedtimes	___ Job pressures
___ Pregnancy	___ Illness
___ Impotence/lack of orgasm	___ Arguments
___ Memories from previous relationships	___ Constant criticism
___ Worries about infertility	
___ Other _____	

What will you do to overcome at least one of these challenges? (Check what you are willing to do within the next two weeks. Be as specific as possible.)

___ Set aside ten minutes a day for intimate conversation —just the two of us.

___ Make love in prime time before we're exhausted. What time is that?

_____

_____

___ Cut back on at least one outside activity. Which one?

49

_____

_____

___ Plan to go out alone each week (breakfast, dinner, coffee, a picnic, a walk, ride in the car, etc.) What will you do?

_____

_____

When?

_____

_____

___ Learn to talk about ourselves with each other. What would you like to talk about?

_____

_____

___ Get rid of distractions. (Turn off TV, put away book or newspaper, spend less time on the phone or with my friends, cut back on a hobby, etc.) What will you do?

_____

_____

___ Go to bed at the same time.

___ Pray together each day—especially pray for the grace of passion in our marriage.

___ Initiate sex more frequently.

_____

___ Do something special just to please you.

___ Help out more around the house. What will you do?

___ Give up pornography.

___ Get professional counseling.

Change is important. All living things are continually changing and evolving. Only we can make changes in ourselves. Spend time together going over your answers and make plans for how you will continue to change and grow together.

Part C: Why Do We Make Love?

Sexual intercourse in marriage is so much more than it is portrayed in movies or love stories. Married love is a treasure house of communications, an opportunity to say with our bodies what we cannot put into words. Sometimes in making love, the couple communicates their feelings of celebration. They've just had a great day, a romantic evening, or a special occasion. You just got a raise, and it's time to celebrate.

Sometimes lovemaking communicates support for one another. When one of you has had a terrible day at work or you've just lost your job or been heavily criticized, making love says to the person, "I believe in you. No matter what happens, I will always love you."

When our self-image is low and we notice we've gained weight, or we're getting gray or wrinkled, making love can say, "I think you're irresistible. To me you are always beautiful."

Hurt feelings can remain after an argument is settled but we can decide to make love even though we don't feel like it. Then lovemaking soothes away the bitter feelings that

51

may linger, the harsh judgments, or the hidden belief, "I know I was right." Lovemaking communicates, "No issue is so great that it will ever divide us. We may not know how to solve this problem at this time, but together we will always work out our problems." Lovemaking can also be healing. In times of pain and deep emotional crisis, such as the death of a loved one, the married couple's lovemaking draws them out of the pain and into the loving reality of each other's arms. Then lovemaking communicates, "I share with you this grief and sorrow. I will never leave you to face your sorrows alone."

Married couples should plan their lovemaking together and not leave it to chance or to when they both feel like it. Make love in prime time—not when you're both exhausted and have little to offer one another. Spend time together just touching and holding each other without making love. Enjoy the beauty and gift of the other person. Be affectionate and thoughtful throughout the day. Don't expect to jump into bed and "turn on."

You don't have to feel like making love in order to make love. Sometimes you won't feel like it, but your husband/wife needs you. Often, once you've begun, you'll start to feel good about it. Always say "yes" to the person, even if you have to say "no" to the action. Make your lives a total "yes" to one another. Be sensitive and caring. Set aside time for just the two of you on a regular, even daily basis.

Sex and sexuality in God's eyes is a gift meant to be used wisely and well by his people. It is a gift that gives new life to the couple in their relationship. It also brings new life into the world in our babies and children.

God intended for men and women to be co-creators with him—to share in the great gift of bringing life into the world. He did this by conferring on husband and wife a love so powerful that it has to have a name—the name you give your child, either by giving birth or adopting.

In some ways, you could say that each child is an outward sign of your love for one another—of the way you loved each other at that time. Just as in all other moral decisions, each couple decides in the total context of their lives when to accept this possibility of having a child. This must be a fully informed decision, and there are a number of issues to be considered.

In the next exercise, reflect on your own attitudes about these issues, and discuss them with your spouse.

* * * * *

Below are a number of possible attitudes about having a family. Put a check mark next to each statement you believe describes your attitude. (You may check more than one statement.)

_____ The commitment to marriage includes the decision to be open to new life. It's a decision I want to discuss now and regularly throughout our marriage.

_____ Any decision to postpone a family should be made only on a temporary basis. It should be a topic that can be reopened at any time by either of us.

_____ Sometimes when couples marry, they both plan to continue full-time with their careers. After the arrival of the first child, however, one or the other may decide to remain at home. Sometimes the other partner then feels cheated because he/she was counting on the extra income. These are decisions we'll discuss often and seriously.

_____ I agree with the research that indicates children benefit greatly when they are cared for by their own parents.

_____ I view children as a burden who will cramp our lifestyle.

_____ Children are a gift from God, a special source of joy and delight. They are also a call to spiritual and emotional growth as we learn the true meaning of selflessness and giving of ourselves to others.

_____ A decision about the number of children we'll have should be thoughtfully and prayerfully considered.

_____ If we choose not to conceive a child at any particular point, it will be an occasion of regret for me.

_____ If we are unable to conceive our own children easily, I would go to extraordinary means to conceive a child.

_____ I would be willing to adopt a child.

Now share your responses with your spouse and discuss them with each other.

You are the only ones who can decide how many children you will have. The ability to bring new life into the world and to nurture the lives of children is a gift from God. It is a source of great joy and great responsibility. Take the time you need, as often as you need, to discuss and pray about your decisions. You may want to meet with your pastor to discuss the issue, and invite him/her to add personal insights to your discussion.

Conclusion

When a married couple is passionately in love with one another, their world and the world of those they touch is a much better place.

The entire atmosphere of the home is transformed when the love of the couple for each other and for God is at its center.

God blesses our sex and sexuality. It is a gift to be used wisely and well; it is a gift that brings joy and peace, not only to the couple, but to the family and community as well.

Throughout time, man and woman have been meant by God to bring life to one another and the earth in order that life may then return again to God. The relationship between a man and a woman is meant to be one of partnership in giving glory to God.

* * * * *

When it comes to having babies, I am the type of person who would ... (Check all that apply.)

_____ Want to have as many as possible.
_____ Be very nervous about the whole thing.
_____ Be concerned about our finances.

___   Look forward to playing with them.
___   Worry about who was going to take care of them.
___   Plan the whole thing very carefully.
___   Tell all my friends immediately.
___   Trust God to be with us.
___   Take on a second job or work overtime to support them.
___   Start planning immediately for their college education.
___   Take one day at a time.
___   *Never* agree to an abortion.
___   Other _____

I think the ideal time for us to start a family is

_____

_____

Now that I realize that we need both intimate conversation as well as sexual intimacy, I feel ...

_____

_____

What do we need to change in order to have prime time together every day?

_____

_____

How can I make my life a total "yes" to you?

_____

_____

When you have both finished writing your responses, share them with each other and talk about them for a few minutes.

When You Question the Roles of Men and Women...

One of the key areas where difficulties arise in marriage is in the roles men and women are expected to play. Years ago these roles were clearly defined by society and largely unquestioned. In general, a man was considered a good husband if he worked hard, didn't drink or spend time in bars or flirt with other women, and brought his paycheck home at the end of the week. A woman was considered a good wife if she kept a clean house and raised the children to be good citizens. Most people assumed that if their roles were fulfilled and the parents also regularly attended church, the couple would have a happy marriage and the children would grow up to be very much like their parents.

Today life is neither so simple nor so ideal. Many men who have fulfilled their roles as providers have found their wives ready to divorce them because they felt lonely and unfulfilled in their relationship. Many wives who are model housekeepers and devoted mothers have been threatened by a discontented husband who finds no joy in their marriage.

We Are Formed by Those Who Raised Us

Much of what you will be in marriage, you bring with you on your wedding day. When you marry, you marry not only one another, you marry your spouse's entire family. It isn't that you move in with your in-laws or even live near each other. You may not even know one another very well. But each of you was formed by the people who raised you. In your childhood you were already developing ideas about what men are like, what women are like and what marriage is all about. It is these attitudes that you bring with you into

56

marriage on your wedding day. They form the background of what you expect your marriage to be like and how you expect each other should behave in order to have a happy marriage.

If a couple has lived together before marriage, it is no guarantee of a happy marriage. In fact, recent data shows that the divorce rate is slightly higher for those who live together before marriage than for those who don't. Expectations for one another change after marriage. Often, behavior that was tolerated in a boyfriend or girlfriend is not tolerated in a husband or wife. It's important, therefore, to discuss the attitudes we each brought to marriage so we'll have few surprises and no hidden agenda about how things "ought to be."

* * * * *

A. Qualities of Men and Women. Go through the list below and put an M next to those qualities you believe are typically masculine and an F next to those you believe are typically feminine. Then go back through the list and put your spouse's initials next to those qualities that best describe him/her.

___ Tender	___ Gentle	___ Kind
___ Ambitious	___ Hardworking	___ Sensitive
___ Intelligent	___ Clever	___ Hardnosed
___ Tough	___ Strong	___ Fearless
___ Childlike	___ Enthusiastic	___ Aggressive
___ Compassionate	___ Generous	___ Trustworthy
___ Cautious	___ Laid back	___ Worldly
___ Helpless	___ Rebellious	___ Happy
___ Perfectionist	___ Organized	___ Slob
___ Athletic	___ Achiever	___ Clown
___ Handles children well	___ Handles money wisely	
___ Good with people	___ Needs tender/loving care	
___ Knows how to run a home	___ Knows the ways of the world	
___ Makes good decisions	___ Selects gifts well	
___ Remembers special occasions	___ Good driver	
___ Gets drunk occasionally	___ Uses drugs	

Which of these qualities do you most admire in your spouse?

_____

_____

Which qualities would you most like to see him/her develop?

_____

_____

B. *Household Chores.* Go through the list below and put a D next to those chores typically done by your dad and an M next to those typically done by your mom. (If you grew up in a single parent household, indicate whether a typical chore was considered a man's or a woman's work—even if your single parent did all the chores.)

MY PARENT'S HOME			OUR HOME		
MOM	DAD		HE	SHE	BOTH
___	___	Buying the groceries	___	___	___
___	___	Cleaning the bathroom	___	___	___
___	___	Planning the meals	___	___	___
___	___	Preparing the meals	___	___	___
___	___	Scrubbing the floor	___	___	___
___	___	Making the beds	___	___	___
___	___	Changing a diaper	___	___	___
___	___	Dusting furniture	___	___	___
___	___	Vacuuming	___	___	___
___	___	Painting a room	___	___	___
___	___	Mowing the lawn	___	___	___
___	___	Inviting friends over	___	___	___
___	___	Caring about family spirituality	___	___	___
___	___	Carrying out the garbage	___	___	___
___	___	Packing lunches	___	___	___

58

__	__	Doing the laundry	__	__	__
__	__	Ironing	__	__	__
__	__	Choosing a house or apartment	__	__	__
__	__	Earning a living	__	__	__
__	__	Deciding where we'll go to have fun	__	__	__
__	__	Planning a vacation	__	__	__
__	__	Paying the bills	__	__	__
__	__	Deciding about insurance policies	__	__	__
__	__	Taking children to doctor/dentist	__	__	__
__	__	Performing household repairs	__	__	__
__	__	Bathing and dressing the children	__	__	__
__	__	Choosing the colors for a room or otherwise decorating the house	__	__	__
__	__	Arranging for a babysitter	__	__	__
__	__	Cleaning up after dinner	__	__	__
__	__	Keeping clothes repaired	__	__	__
__	__	Caring for a sick child	__	__	__
__	__	Responding to a child in the middle of the night	__	__	__
__	__	Looking after elderly relatives	__	__	__
__	__	Visiting a sick person	__	__	__
__	__	Going to a funeral home	__	__	__
__	__	Buying gifts for the family	__	__	__
__	__	Baking	__	__	__
__	__	Involved in community activities	__	__	__
__	__	Involved in school activities of children	__	__	__

—	—	Discipline of children	—	—	—
—	—	Played with children	—	—	—
—	—	Openly affectionate	—	—	—

Now go back through the list and put a check mark in the appropriate column (HE, SHE, BOTH) to indicate how you want to divide household chores in your own home.

How will your attitude about the division of household chores change if either one of you remains at home full-time for some period of time?

_____

_____

Put a * next to all those chores you would expect your spouse to take over completely.

C. In your family who had the final word about how the family money would be spent?

_____

_____

Who usually paid the family bills?

_____

_____

How would you like these chores divided in your home?

_____

_____

D. In your family, who was most likely to discipline the children?

_____

_____

Was the discipline in the form of hitting/slapping, yelling, grounding, reasoning, or other?

_____

_____

How do you expect to discipline your own children?

_____

_____

Who will do it?

_____

_____

E. How often did your family get together with their extended family (parents, brothers and sisters, in-laws, etc.)?

_____

_____

How often do you plan to see your own family?

_____

_____

How often do you plan to see your spouse's family?

_____

F. What role did alcohol play in your family?

___	Never allowed	___	A drink was a nightly ritual
___	Only dad drank	___	Only mom drank
___	Wine at meals	___	Both parents drank moderately

___ Alcohol at parties and family gatherings
___ Alcohol was restricted only to adults over twenty-one
___ Sometimes children were allowed a small amount of alcohol
___ Either/both parents would get drunk occasionally
___ Either/both parents drank when they went out
___ Either/both parents were often at a bar
___ Either/both parents were alcoholics

Go through the list above and put a * next to those items that best describe the role you expect alcohol/drugs to play in your marriage.

What role do alcohol/drugs play in your relationship with your spouse now?

_____

_____

Is there any change you would like your spouse to make now either in attitude about, or use of, alcohol/drugs?

_____

_____

What changes are you willing to make in your use of alcohol/drugs?

_____

_____

G. What role do drugs play in your life?

HE   SHE

HE	SHE	
___	___	Has never used drugs.
___	___	No longer uses drugs.
___	___	Has had drug counseling.
___	___	Still uses drugs occasionally.
___	___	Experiences financial difficulty because of drug use.
___	___	Needs counseling for drugs.
___	___	Needs to change attitudes/habits about drugs.
___	___	Does drugs alone or with friends.
___	___	Does drugs with me.
___	___	Thinks drug habits are under control
___	___	Still sometimes crave drugs.
___	___	Uses drugs to escape from problems or life.
___	___	Does drugs to keep the other person company.
___	___	Has been hospitalized for drug abuse.

Do you see the use of drugs as part of your future together?

_____

_____

Do you see a need for counseling for you or your spouse?

_____

_____

H. Do you plan to have a separate night out with the girls/guys?

_____

_____

How often?

_____

Do your friends add to or detract from your relationship as a couple?

_____

_____

Are there some friends you believe are harmful to your relationship?

_____

_____

Who are they?

_____

_____

Would either one or both of you be willing to change friends to please one another?

_____

_____

Which friends would you be willing to change?

_____

_____

Do you expect your friends to drop by unannounced?

_____

Do you have good friends who are couples?

_____

Are you willing/able to form new friendships with other couples?

_____

I. Are you both planning to work after marriage? _____
   How long do you plan to work? Husband _____
                                   Wife _____
   If you had to choose between careers, whose career would you say is most important?   Husband _____
                                   Wife _____
   If one of you was offered a better job out of town, would you be willing to give up your own job to follow your spouse?

_____

If you have a baby, whom would you expect to stay home to care for the child?
___ Husband   ___ Wife   ___ Neither of us
Whom would you see as child-care provider in your absence?

_____

After both of you have written your responses to all the Exercises above, share them with each other and discuss those items, in depth, which strike you as especially meaningful in your relationship.

Wrap-Up

In every marriage there are issues that can divide us. Some issues, like drug and alcohol abuse and physical and verbal abuse, are very serious and must be dealt with. If either of you has a history of abusive behavior toward yourself or others and you have not received counseling, serious consideration must be given to counseling and changed behavior before marriage. Marriage is not going to solve a serious problem or change negative behavior into positive behavior.

It's impossible to surface all the underlying attitudes and issues that may exist between a couple. It is hoped that these lists helped to clarify a few issues and brought to the surface any major differences you may have. Be sure to take the time you need to discuss any potential areas of disagreement.

Feel free to consult your pastor or a professional counselor if necessary to help you resolve any issues you cannot work through on your own. It's important to both of you that you face up to all the areas of your lives, even those that are most difficult to talk about, and deal with them before they become a major issue that destroys the trust and confidence of your marriage.

When You're Discussing Money . . .

There is a purpose to life—and the purpose is not to become rich or successful or famous. That may happen, but that's not the goal. The goal of every Christian is to love God and love our neighbor here on earth and to reach heaven when we die.

Yet for many of us, the goal of life becomes confused with the goals of our society and the pressures of supporting ourselves and our families. We also live with the silent, often unspoken expectations of our hopes and dreams for what our life ought to be. Once children arrive, we add to that our own desire to offer our children a wonderful life—filled with joy, laughter, great experiences, toys and games, a good education, and everything that we never had. As Christians in a materialistic society it's difficult to sort out the proper role of money and to keep our real goals in mind. Let's look at some of the advice we receive.

* * * * *

In the appropriate column below put a check mark next to any of the ideas that affect you now or have done so in the past. Then go back through and check any that you believe your spouse accepts.

HUSBAND   WIFE
___   You Can Have It All!   ___
___   If You Want It, Buy It!   ___
___   Reach Out and Touch Someone.   ___
___   Last Chance! Never Again Values Like This!   ___
___   The One Who Dies with the Most Toys Wins.   ___
___   The Loving Father Provides ...   ___
___   Don't Let Your Family Go Unprotected!   ___

___ You Deserve a Break Today ...	___
___ Don't Wait! Get What You Want Today!	___
___ Your Home Reflects Your Good Taste	___
___ Clothes Make the Man/Woman	___
___ What Will the Neighbors Think?	___
___ This Is Your Last Chance To Get In on This Deal!	___
___ This Opportunity To Invest Won't Come Around Again!	___
___ Have We Got a Deal for You!	___
___ Clearance Sale! Unheard-of Bargains! Everything Reduced!	___
___ Buy Now...Pay Later.	___
___ Why Should You Wait for What You Really Want and Need?	___
___ Protect Your Family Now with ...	___
___ Own the Home of Your Dreams.	___
___ A Penny Saved Is a Penny Earned.	___
___ You Too Can Win the Big Prize!	___
___ You Are a Certified Winner of Our Sweepstakes ___	

While none of these statements is harmful in itself, how do they influence your dreams and expectations? Put your initial next to those items that describe you.

___ Not at all.
___ I wish I had more money to spend.
___ I feel guilty when I can't provide more.
___ I am embarrassed by what we have.
___ I'm afraid that others judge us by the way we look.
___ I'm envious of those who have more.
___ I dream of things we'll probably never have.
___ I work hard to get all we want and need.
___ I feel responsible for my family's well-being.
___ I find it almost impossible to save.
___ I can't resist a bargain—even if we can't afford it.
___ I spend a lot to make others happy.
___ My family expects us to have things.
___ I go for instant gratification—even if I have to charge it!

____ I buy nice gifts to show people how much I love them.
____ I see a need for both of us to work to get ahead.
____ It's important to me to have more than my parents had.
____ I'd like to have as much as my parents had.
____ I sometimes see myself as a failure in handling money.
____ I really don't enjoy money or the things it can buy.
____ I need financial security.
____ We'll limit the size of our family so we can have more possessions.
____ I'll never have anything because I spend what I have.
____ I believe we should save at least _____
____ Other _____

Now go back through the list and put your spouse's initial next to those items that best describe his/her attitudes.

Put your initial next to the description that best describes how you feel about spending money. Then put your spouse's initial next to the item that best describes him/her.

____ Spender—Feels alive and free when spending money.
____ Avoider—Never keeps track of money or checkbook balance.
____ Worrier—Continually worries about how much money we have.
____ Saver—Feels secure and safe when saving and budgeting.
____ Idealist—Refuses to be practical about how much money we need to do what we want.
____ Planner—Needs detailed plans for the future.
____ Purist—Sees money as a source of evil and never enjoys it.
____ Developer—Wants to accumulate as much money as possible.
How does this affect our relationship?

_____

_____

How can we change our attitudes and behavior to make life better for both of us?

_____

_____

Discuss your answers with one another. What are your similarities? What are your differences? How are each of you influenced by society? How have you forced one another to take on a role you'd rather not have? (The big spender forces the other to be a saver or worrier.) How does this affect your relationship? How can you change your attitudes and behavior to make life better for both of you?

The Family's Influence

Although all of us are affected by the cultural values of our society, perhaps the most powerful influence comes from our family. The attitudes we have about money—how it should be spent or saved, or what constitutes a necessary expense or a foolish waste of money, or whether we should pay our bills on time or whether we can postpone them—most often come from the home in which we were raised.

If we have fond memories of lavish Christmas gifts and wonderful vacations, we'll probably want to duplicate them. If we have bitter memories of quarreling over money or deep poverty, we'll probably want to avoid that. Sometimes our memories of money and how it was spent—or not spent—are so powerful that we find it almost impossible to communicate with or listen to our spouse. We each know we are right! Therefore it's helpful to understand how each of us came to have our opinions.

In some families the material success of the children is considered a mark of success for the parents and a source of pride. This puts an added burden on a young couple to be materially successful, not for their own sake, but for the sake of their family.

No matter how rich or how poor our family was, they

had definite attitudes about money, credit, savings, insurance, security, and possessions. Let's look at some of the attitudes your family had and some of those you have today.

* * * * *

Put a check mark in the column on the left for each item that describes your family's attitude about handling money. Then go back through the list and put a check mark in the right-hand column for each item that describes your attitude now.

MY FAMILY'S ATTITUDE		MY ATTITUDE NOW
___	Money should be saved on a regular basis.	___
___	If you have money in your pocket, you'll probably spend it.	___
___	If you see what you like, you should get it.	___
___	Money is no problem.	___
___	It's important to have good insurance.	___
___	Charge cards are dangerous.	___
___	It's best to keep your finances a secret—even from each other.	___
___	Sometimes it's necessary to have a secret savings account.	___
___	Women/men can't be trusted with money.	___
___	All our money should be pooled in a common fund.	___
___	Both of us should have our own spending money	___
___	No one has the right to tell me how to spend the money I earn.	___
___	It's important to give to church/charity.	___
___	We are "smart money" people.	___
___	One of us is superior to the other in handling money.	___
___	Money is meant to be spent.	___
___	If you can't have fun with your money, there's no point in working.	___
___	Live today—pay tomorrow!	___
___	It's best to keep a husband's/wife's money separate.	___

71

___	Money is difficult to get. It must be handled carefully.	___
___	I am more likely to be more responsible with money.	___
___	We never talk about money.	___
___	Money is the source of many arguments.	___
___	Children should not be informed about family financial problems.	___
___	Money is the root of all evil.	___
___	If we can get what we want without working, why work?	___
___	God helps those who help themselves.	___
___	Charity begins at home.	___
___	Other_____	___

Each of us also has priorities about how our money should be spent. In fact, a major cause of arguments among married couples is not how much money they have, but how the money they have will be spent. Let's look again at some family attitudes about priorities and your own attitudes about how you want to spend your money.

* * * * *

In the left-hand column, put a number 1 next to the item your family of origin would list as a top priority in budgeting money each month. Then go back through the list and put a 2 next to second priority, a 3 next to third priority, etc. If the item wouldn't even be considered in the family budget, put a zero next to it. Do the same thing for your own priorities today in the right-hand column.

FAMILY PRIORITIES		MY PRIORITIES
___	Food	___
___	Medicine	___
___	Dental care	___
___	Medical care (check-ups, vaccines, eye glasses, etc.)	___
___	Beauty/grooming (haircuts, make-up, nails, etc.)	___
___	Entertainment	___

___	Clothing	___
___	Rent/mortgage	___
___	Saving for something we really want	___
___	Savings/investments for the future	___
___	Insurance	___
___	Utility bills (phone, electric, heat, etc.)	___
___	Automobile	___
___	Vacations	___
___	Alcohol, drugs, etc.	___
___	College education (our own or our children's)	___
___	Tuition in a Christian grammar/high school	___
___	Toys for children	___
___	Adult hobbies	___
___	Physical fitness equipment	___
___	Membership in clubs/organizations	___
___	Books/magazines	___
___	Musical instruments/lessons	___
___	Charities	___
___	Church offering	___
___	Electronic equipment	___
___	Gifts (for ourselves or others)	___
___	Furniture	___
___	Household expenses (cleaning supplies, repairs, etc.)	___
___	Other_____	___

How much money are you and your spouse currently spending on each of the items listed? Write down the amounts in each category. (You will probably have to get together to establish this.)

Separately decide how much you believe you should be spending for each item. Compare your answers.

Are you spending more than you earn?

         ___ Yes   ___ No

Are you realistic in your expectations about how far your money will go?   ___ Yes   ___ No

If you are spending less than you earn, what's happening with the extra money? Is it going into a mutual savings account or for something you both want?

      ___ Yes   ___ No

Do you both agree that your spending is right on target?

      ___ Yes   ___ No

How can you adjust your spending/saving to please both of you, at least to some extent?

_____

_____

Do you basically trust your spouse with your money?

      ___ Yes   ___ No

Wrap-Up

The best way to get control of money is to write a budget that you both can agree on. Most banks or credit unions offer booklets to help you plan a budget. With some couples money is such a hot topic that they need to sit down with someone else to help them sort out their priorities. For others, particularly those in deep debt, it's advisable to consult an expert to help you regain control of your finances. Your pastor should be able to help you find a dependable person to assist you.

Money as Power

Money is a necessity, and money is power. That's true in society; it's also true in the home. The one who controls the money and handles the budget is most often the one who has that power. That's the person who most readily can say, "Yes, we will buy this," or "No, we can't have that." Without knowledge or access to the budget, the other partner can't present a reasonable case for an expenditure. The one who controls the budget also is the one most likely to put money away in secret places—a few dollars here or there to save for something special he/she wants. The person without control often has no idea these funds exist and therefore has little or no say in their distribution.

Another power game between partners occurs as each tries to get what he/she wants. Perhaps they both agree that one income is their main source of funds for household and living expenses. Often the partner who is earning less or working part-time declares his/her income untouchable. It's being spent for special projects that person deems most important.

Sometimes the partner without access to family funds takes power by using credit cards or writing checks to get what he/she wants. While one partner deems new purchases off-limits, the other continues to spend. Even if that person lacks transportation to stores, he/she shops by phone or catalogue.

There is no end to the games we play to get what we want. This behavior, however, only erodes trust and confidence in a relationship. We need to eliminate the games, approach one another in honesty and trust, pray to God for guidance, and decide together in prayer how to spend the money we have where it will do the most good for ourselves and others. Jesus continually warned his followers about the proper use of money. As Christians, we are *obliged* to live simply, spend responsibly, and share with those who have less.

When You're Worried About Your In-Laws . . .

Just about everyone has heard and read jokes about the relationship with in-laws—especially jokes about mothers-in-law. Coming from a society that often assumes there will be trouble and negative intervention in a young couple's private affairs from in-laws, it's easy to assume a hostile or defensive position when dealing with your spouse's parents.

Yet the fourth commandment tells us: "Honor your father and your mother, as the Lord your God commanded you, so that your days may be long and that it may go well with you in the land that the Lord your God is giving you" (Dt 5:16).

While we often hear these words directed at children, they were originally intended for the relationship between adults and their parents.

In a beautiful passage in the book of Tobit, we read the words of one father, Raguel, to his daughter, Sarah, who is about to depart with Tobias, her new husband for the home of her in-laws. Raguel embraces his son-in-law and says to the young couple: "'Farewell, my child; have a safe journey. The Lord of heaven prosper you and your wife Sarah, and may I see children of yours before I die.' Then he kissed his daughter Sarah and said to her, 'My daughter, honor your father-in-law and your mother-in-law, since from now on they are as much your parents as those who gave you birth. Go in peace, daughter, and may I hear a good report about you as long as I live.' Then he bade them farewell and let them go" (Tob 10:11-12).

The relationship between young adult children and their parents ideally is meant to bring strength and comfort to both.

It's often true, however, that first impressions are difficult for all concerned. Parents have hopes and dreams for their children. They want them to finish school, get a good job, and marry just the right person. Many parents dream of their child's future even more than the child does, and they have definite opinions about how it should go. Because of these hopes and expectations, they may put pressure on both of you to do things their way.

Maybe you fulfilled all the expectations both your families had for your wedding and maybe you didn't. Maybe you hit it off with your in-laws immediately, and maybe they're still not sure they like you. Maybe you're dealing with a traditional two-parent family of in-laws, or maybe you have the more complicated role of loving your spouse's stepparents or their boyfriend/girlfriend. Whatever your situation, there are a few simple things to keep in mind as you enter into these relationships.

How To Relate to In-Laws

1. *Expect the best.* Most parents are good people and wish only the best for their children. They may not understand you, your values or your ideas, especially in the early years of your marriage, but approach them with the love and trust with which you approached their son or daughter on your first date. Listen to them with a sympathetic ear and give them the benefit of the doubt. Try not to judge them or attribute to them evil motives.

2. *If you want your parent(s) to love and accept your spouse, don't constantly complain about him/her.* You may be just getting it off your chest. They are probably thinking you are in an unhappy marriage. Also, don't complain about your spouse to his/her own parents or family. That's a sure way to get them to reject you.

3. *Remember that you are not in competition with your in-laws for your spouse's love and affection.* When you chose to marry one another, you were making a public statement of your love and commitment to each other as a first priority for both of you. This is not to say that you no longer love your parents, but it is saying that your own relationship has a higher priority than all others. Therefore, you can afford to

be generous and kind with your in-laws—especially if you are working on your couple relationship and receiving the attention and love you need from one another.

4. *Try to distribute yourselves as equally as possible among both families, spending time and attention on both.* Sometimes it's impossible to be completely equal, but make the time to visit, especially for holidays and special occasions. When one set of in-laws is honored and the other is resented or cut off, there is bound to be hurt among them and competition for your attention. It's also important to remember both sets of parents on birthdays, anniversaries, etc. Sometimes one of you will be better at this than the other, but it should be a "couple" effort as much as possible. Mark your calendar for the whole year because you'll probably never remember all the dates. Then you should both check ahead each month so you'll be prepared to call, write or send a card.

5. *Sometimes these relationships are awkward because we don't know what to call our in-laws.* Ask them. They probably have a preference for how they wish to be addressed. Some parents like to be called simply mom and dad. Others like to be called by their first names. It helps to clarify little things early, before difficulties set in.

6. *In-laws are like anyone else.* They want to be treated with respect—just as you do. A mature, adult relationship is possible between parents and children. It should be natural to go to both sets of parents for advice about your important decisions. Often parents only want to be consulted; once they have their say, most are willing to back off to let you make your own decisions as a couple. On the other hand, if you never consult them, they may feel offended that you don't care about their opinion and become pushy and overbearing just to make sure they are heard. Ultimately, of course, all decisions must be made by the two of you. Having consulted your parents as well as other experts, you should be able to make informed decisions.

7. *Part of a mature relationship is to recognize that people don't always have to agree on the issues in order to love and respect one another.* It's essential to forgive your own parents and your in-laws for any mistakes they have made

in the past. Parents aren't perfect; you probably realized that when you were a teenager. But assume they did the best they could with what they had and what they understood as their child's needs and desires.

In extreme cases, where there has been abuse, get the counseling you need so you don't carry over into marriage the sorrow and pain of the past. To forgive does not mean that everything that happened is all right nor does it mean you will now welcome a difficult or abusive parent to live with you. It does mean that you are leaving the judgment of others up to God and that you are getting on with your life.

8. *Welcome your in-laws into your home to visit.* Most parents desperately want to be loved and accepted by their sons- and daughters-in-law. You may have to set down guidelines to establish whether parents should phone before they come and how long they should stay when they visit. In most cases, when there is a problem, it's best if the son deals with his parents and the daughter with her parents. The bonds of affection have already been well established in these relationships and difficult news is more likely to be accepted from their own child. If there is a difference of opinion, it can be handled then rather than left to linger for months or years on end.

9. *Your parents and your in-laws can be valuable sources of encouragement and support to your marriage and family, not only in the early years, but throughout your lives.* Many in-laws have experience to share, skills to offer, love to give, and a generous spirit of self-giving, particularly when the grandchildren arrive. Good parents are a gift from God and you are well blessed if you have them. Take the time to thank God for your parents, and, if possible, invite your parents to pray with you and your children.

Your in-laws can shed light on who your spouse is, what that person was like as a child, the values and ideas that were shared. As you get to know them better, you'll begin to observe the family traits and the family style of doing things. Together you can talk about these things. How do they affect your relationship? What can you learn from your in-laws—both positive and negative? What do they do that you would like to duplicate? What would you both choose to eliminate? Discuss the traditions of both families, keep some of both, and blend in your own ideas. Remember, whether they are wonderful people and easy for you to love or difficult people who constantly challenge you, they are the first people who loved your spouse and they must have done at least a few things right to have produced such a wonderful person for you to marry.

Ultimately, of course, you are not in control of whether or not your in-laws love and accept you. It's important, then, to remember that God is not asking us to change other people. God is only asking us to love them. You can do that—even if you have to do it from a distance.

Here are a few questions to help you in your discussion with your spouse.

* * * * *

What beautiful qualities do I see in you that I believe came from your family? (Check all that apply and add your own.)

___	Easygoing temperament	___	Inner peace
___	Prayerfulness	___	Deep faith
___	Openness	___	Sense of adventure
___	Hope	___	Charity
___	Patience	___	Kindness
___	Enthusiasm	___	Inner strength
___	Ambition	___	Willingness to work hard
___	Love for family	___	Physical skills
___	Sense of commitment	___	Love for children
___	Desire to help others	___	Idealism
___	Other _____		

What do I like best about your relationship with your parent(s)?

_____

_____

What do I like best about my relationship with my parent(s)?

_____

_____

What traditions, values or ideals are present in your family that I would like to have in our home?

_____

_____

What traditions, values or ideals do we have in my family that I would like to have in our home?

_____

_____

If there were one thing in either of our families that I would not like to duplicate in our marriage, it would be ...

_____

_____

The way you can help me grow closer to your family is ...

_____

_____

The way I would like to help my family grow closer to you is ...

_____

_____

When You're Not Feeling Well . . .

Most people take their health for granted—until the day comes when they don't feel well. Then they are often accused of becoming "another person," a "big baby" or an "irritable grouch." Whether the illness is an ordinary case of the flu or the sudden onset of a major disease, illness affects not only the way we feel, but the way we think and experience life and relate to our spouse.

Illness can deprive us of a sense of humor, take away our hope for a better tomorrow, cast us into deep despair, and totally frustrate us. The caregiver may find himself/herself alternately tender and gentle with the patient or annoyed and angry about the whole situation. It's a time when we need to understand one another more—and to work together to make the best of a difficult time in our lives.

Abusing Our Bodies

In 1 Corinthians 6:19-20 we read: "Do you not know that your body is a temple of the Holy Spirit within you, which you have from God, and that you are not your own? For you were bought with a price; therefore glorify God in your body."

St. Paul exhorts us to live lives of purity and wholeness, using our bodies to give honor and glory to God. Too often we take our bodies for granted and use or abuse them in overwork, overexertion or overextending ourselves. Our society values the over-achiever.

Most people fail to see their bodies as St. Paul did—as sacred vessels, literally temples of the Holy Spirit. Some people abuse their bodies in other ways—giving in to over-indulgence and excesses that cause physical harm. St. Paul invites us to think of our bodies in new ways and to treat them with reverence and respect. As a husband and wife, you have become a new body together. There is a oneness between you that is so profound that what you do to your own body has a lifelong impact on your spouse. You are no longer "your own person." You belong to one another now and you have a stake in the emotional and physical well-being of each other.

Because each of us is different in our approach to life, it's necessary to understand one another in the whole area of health and sickness. The following questions may help to get you started in your discussions.

* * * * *

A. When you are feeling well, are you the kind of person who ... (check all that apply to you)?

HE	SHE	
___	___	Takes very good care of yourself.
___	___	Lives in fear of getting sick.
___	___	Exercises regularly.
___	___	Takes vitamins.
___	___	Is willing to get a check-up even when you're not sick.
___	___	Takes your health for granted.
___	___	Indulges in at least one or two bad habits.
___	___	Expects your spouse to feel as good as you do.
___	___	Feels a lot of sympathy for someone who is sick.
___	___	Avoids sickness or sick people as much as possible.
___	___	Tends to be a couch potato.
___	___	Resists having anyone tell you what to do.
___	___	Watches your diet.
___	___	Other_____

Now go back through the list and put a * next to all those items that best describe your spouse.

B. When you are feeling ill, are you the kind of person who ... (check all that apply to you)?

HE	SHE	
——	——	Toughs it out.
——	——	Never gives in to illness.
——	——	Is willing to see a doctor.
——	——	Refuses to see a doctor.
——	——	Prefers to be left alone.
——	——	Appreciates extra attention.
——	——	Expects to be babied.
——	——	Wallows in self-pity.
——	——	Wouldn't dream of missing work.
——	——	Will take a few days of rest.
——	——	Would like help with household chores.
——	——	Won't ask for help even if you need it.
——	——	Buries yourself in TV or a book.
——	——	Tries to "sleep it off."
——	——	Needs someone else to give you permission to be sick.
——	——	Feels frustrated if the illness lasts more than two or three days.
——	——	Wants someone to pray for you.
——	——	Other_____

Now go back through the list and put a * next to all those that apply to your spouse.

C. When you are sick, what would you like your spouse to do for you? (Answer Yes or No.)

YES	NO	
——	——	Call my boss to say I'll be out of work.
——	——	Tell me it's okay to go to bed and rest.
——	——	Get me to the doctor or hospital even if I don't want to go.
——	——	Leave me absolutely alone.
——	——	Take all our phone calls for a few days.
——	——	Bring me my medicine.
——	——	Take over cooking and household chores.
——	——	Forgive me if I'm irritable.
——	——	Bring me flowers or special treats.
——	——	Give me a massage.
——	——	Make sure I'm comfortable.

HE	SHE	
___	___	Sit and talk with me.
___	___	Be patient with me.
___	___	Make love with me.
___	___	Pray over me.
___	___	Other_____

Now go back through the list and put a * next to those things you are willing to do for your spouse when your spouse is sick.

When you have both finished writing your responses, share them with each other and discuss them for at least fifteen minutes. Then proceed with the next exercise.

* * * * *

In marriage our bodies do not belong solely to ourselves. We belong to each other. The way we use or abuse our bodies ultimately will affect our marriage and perhaps our whole way of life. We owe it to one another to listen to what our spouse is telling us about our health.

* * * * *

A. Below are some possible areas of concern about the way health is cared for (put a checkmark next to all those that describe you or your spouse).

HE	SHE	
___	___	Drinking, particularly heavy drinking.
___	___	Use of drugs.
___	___	Chronic fatigue.
___	___	Smoking.
___	___	Chronic stress and anxiety.
___	___	Poor eating habits—overeating or constant dieting.
___	___	Deliberately eating foods that are unhealthy or disagree with you.
___	___	Bulimia or anorexia.
___	___	Chronic allergies.
___	___	Physical inactivity.
___	___	Compulsive activity.
___	___	Overwork.

85

		Lack of rest.
___	___	Other_____

B. Answer the questions below as honestly as possible.
What habit does your spouse have that you would like changed?

_____

_____

What habit do you have that you know you need to change?

_____

_____

What steps will you take now to begin to correct this habit?

_____

_____

Now share your responses with your spouse and talk about them for at least fifteen minutes.

Conclusion

The only person you can change is yourself. All changes must begin within. The rules for good health are well known and with some discipline are easily followed. They include a well-balanced diet, exercise, and a well-balanced life that includes work, play, prayer, and time for rest. In addition, you may have particular health needs that must be met in order to maximize your life span and your health. Working together, you can be a source of enthusiasm and encouragement for one another that will keep you going and growing together for a lifetime.

When You Want To Talk About God . . .

When a couple comes to the church for their marriage, they are implying that God is important in their lives. They want their marriage to be blessed by God. They desire to have God in their relationship, not just on their wedding day, but in all the days and years that lie ahead.

For some engaged couples, the focus is not on God, but only on their plans for a beautiful wedding and a lovely reception and honeymoon. The fact that you chose to come to the church for your marriage is symbolic of the religious training and background either or both of you may share and of your desire to build a strong foundation for your marriage.

Whether we are aware of it or not, when we are open to lifelong committed love, we are also open to God's love. Listen to what we read in scripture from 1 John 4:7-12: "Beloved, let us love one another, because love is from God; everyone who loves is born of God and knows God. Whoever does not love does not know God, for God is love. God's love was revealed among us in this way: God sent his only Son into the world so that we might live through him. In this is love, not that we loved God but that he loved us and sent his Son to be the atoning sacrifice for our sins. Beloved, since God loved us so much, we also ought to love one another. No one has ever seen God; if we love one another, God lives in us, and his love is perfected in us."

God loves us so much that he sent his Son as the sacrifice for our sins. When Jesus came, he revealed his Father as total love. Few people will experience God's love directly in mystical visions, inner voices, or insights. The way most people experience God's love, compassion, forgiveness, and understanding is in the love we share with one another, especially in marriage and family.

When we live in love, we not only fulfill God's command to love one another, but we also make God's love come alive here on earth. Love originates in God and goes out through us to one another. In Christian marriage we have an awesome and wonderful responsibility.

Experiencing God

Since God is the essence of love and at the heart of what we are all about as a couple, it is essential to understand how each of us knows and experiences God in our own lives. It's also important to know what to expect from one another in the years ahead about how each plans to grow in love and knowledge of God. The next exercise will help us focus on some of these questions.

* * * * *

A. When you think of God, what images come to your mind? (Check all that apply.)

___	Wise old man.	___	Harsh judge.
___	Scorekeeper of good and evil.	___	A mother figure.
___	The ten commandments.	___	A father figure.
___	A Being of total love.	___	Creator of all.
___	One who inspires love in me.		
___	One who inspires fear in me.		
___	I don't believe in God.		
___	I've never really thought about God.		
___	I'd like to know more about God.		
___	Other _____		

(What other ways would you describe God or your relationship to him?)

_____

_____

B. The following are words that have sometimes been used
   to describe Jesus. How would you describe Jesus? (Check
   all that apply.)

___ Gentle.	___ Kind.
___ Compassionate.	___ A healer.
___ Our Savior.	___ The crucified.
___ Redeemer.	___ Demanding.
___ My personal Savior.	___ A friend.
___ A brother.	___ A trouble-maker.
___ The Messiah.	___ A prophet.
___ A stranger to me.	___ Not important to me.
___ Challenging.	___ Teacher.

___ I have a personal relationship with Jesus.
___ I don't feel close to Jesus.
___ I don't know much about Jesus or his teachings.
___ I want to know more about Jesus.
___ I don't believe in Jesus.
___ Other _____

   (What other ways would you describe Jesus or your
   relationship to him?)

_____

_____

C. The following is a list of religious attitudes and practices.
   Go through the list and check off all those that apply to
   you.

___ I believe that going to church every Sunday is
   important for us.
___ I want to make God the center of our home and our
   love.
___ I believe it is important to have outward signs of our
   faith in our home (a cross or other religious symbols).
   The most significant religious symbol to me is

   _____

   I would like to have this symbol in our home.
                              ___ Yes ___ No
___ I believe it's important to pray every day.

_____ I pray every day.
_____ I would like us to pray together. How often?

_____

_____

_____ I believe that if we say we love God, we must also
keep his commands.
_____ I believe in God, but I don't believe that any
particular religious practice is necessary.
_____ I don't believe in God and don't intend to practice any
religion.
_____ I'm angry with God.
_____ I enjoy spiritual reading (i.e. Christian books,
magazines, journals, etc.).
_____ I would like you to continue to practice your faith
throughout our marriage.
_____ I would eventually like us to become members of the
same faith community.
_____ I believe all things are God's gifts to us.
_____ I believe God knows and loves each of us intimately.
_____ I believe knowing and understanding the Bible is
important.
I would like to attend Bible study classes.
                              _____ Yes   _____ No
_____ I find God's presence everywhere.
_____ I believe God helped us find each other.
_____ I believe God blesses our love.
_____ As a child I studied religion.
_____ I want our children to study religion.
_____ I believe baptism is important.
_____ I want our children to be baptized.
In what faith community?

_____

_____

_____ I believe there is life after death.

___ I hope to spend eternity with God in heaven.
___ I don't believe in life after death.
___ I believe it is important to have friends with whom we can share our faith.
___ I believe that if we are really living our faith, we probably won't always fit in with what others are doing in our society.
___ I believe it is important to avoid doing things which may hurt someone else or myself.
___ I believe we are called to forgive those who hurt us.
___ I try to forgive everyone who has hurt me.
___ I believe God will help us overcome any temptations that would destroy our marriage.
___ I believe we can make God's love real to one another.
___ I believe we can help one another get to heaven.
___ I believe it is important to be involved in church activities beyond Sunday services.
___ I will teach our children to pray, and I will pray with them.
___ I will respect your religious beliefs and encourage you to practice your faith.
___ I will help you find time to pray each day.
___ I am willing to continue to talk to you about our religious beliefs.
___ I am willing to respect any differences we may have in our beliefs.
___ I will avoid any sense of religious superiority over you.

Compare your answers with one another. Take your time and go over them carefully—listening with your heart. If you wish, begin your discussion with a prayer and invite God to be with you as you discuss this most intimate part of your lives together.

For many couples, their relationship with God is a powerful bond that unites them even when they have difficulties or experience great sorrow or suffering. In fact, with couples who have deep faith, their suffering can draw them closer to God and to one another. For others, their religious beliefs are a difficult topic; they seldom or never discuss them. As a result, they often experience loneliness and misunderstanding in this area.

One person may pray and practice a religious faith, while the other slips away from any involvement. One may be forced to become the spiritual head of the household, responsible for the spiritual needs of the entire family. This can lead to great resentment.

For some, religious practices are such a hot topic that they refuse to discuss the issue. They're afraid of rocking the boat. Sometimes this leads to religious indifference on both persons' part. They practice no religion, seldom or never pray, do not read the Bible, and live only for the moment. But this is like burying your head in the sand.

Sooner or later every person has to face the issues of life and death. How we see and experience God greatly influences the way we will respond to all our difficulties and challenges in life. We must talk about our relationship with God and church and work toward unity as much as possible—understanding our differences and emphasizing our similarities.

When We're Living the Covenant...

A Christian marriage invites us to enter into the mystery of Christ's love—a love so rich and so passionate that he was willing to die for us. While most of us will never be asked to die for our beloved, we will often have to die to ourselves, our self-will, our selfishness, in order to consider the good of the other and of our relationship. We are not talking about giving up or giving in; we are simply talking about total giving of ourselves to one another.

The cross is a rich and powerful symbol of God's love for us. It is also a powerful symbol of married love. We will be one another's greatest blessing and also one another's greatest cross. St. Paul tells us that in a Christian marriage the couple's witness of their love for one another becomes a sign of how much Christ loves the church. We can't actually see Jesus' love—his spiritual union with each one of us. However, we can see the love of a man and a woman for one another. We can experience it, be part of it, enjoy it, and bask in the warmth of a love that grows stronger day by day, month by month and year by year.

It's not the unrealistic love of two unreal, perfect people who never have an argument or disagreement between them, but the love of real, imperfect people who are willing to understand one another's shortcomings and work on *changing themselves* to be considerate of the other and grow toward perfection in the eyes of God.

The process of living out a Christian marriage is much more than just fulfilling a number of obligations. It involves taking the person I love and making him/her part of my very identity. It means that my spouse will be my first priority—above all others, including the members of my own family. I will take your feelings, your values, your ideas into consideration before I make any decisions.

On a practical level this will include everything from the type of coffee we'll put in the coffeemaker every morning, to whether or not we'll accept an out-of-town job, to where we'll have our next holiday dinner. By our baptism we are called to be agents of God's love in many ways. Through our married love we will bring God's love not only to one another, but to the entire faith community—as well as those with whom we live and work.

This is the covenant of Christian marriage. It is a commitment of the couple to each other and to the Christian community to love one another forever and to work on their relationship throughout their lives—"in good times and in bad," and to represent their faith community through the witness of their married love. It is also a commitment of the faith community to love and support the married couple throughout their lives in whatever way the couple needs assistance—"in good times and in bad." Both the faith community and the couple are saying yes to the marriage vows. The couple promises to model the love of Jesus to the whole community. The community promises to model the love of Jesus to the couple. The marriage covenant is much more than a contract. Every contract has conditions that can make the contract null and void.

The covenant made by Jesus Christ has no conditions. It is a total commitment. Since none of us knows what the future has in store, it's frightening to think of entering into such a covenant. That's why we have each other and the whole community. That's why we have our faith in God to love and guide all of us and remain with us throughout our lives. In our marriage covenant, we place ourselves totally in God's hands. God will never fail us.

Jesus made many promises to his followers. We don't always experience these promises, but even when things are difficult, and we aren't aware of it, the promises still stand.

In order to get a closer understanding of how we are to live out our Christian marriage, let's look at how Jesus loves his church. What are the qualities of his covenant with us?

1. *Jesus' love is persevering.*
    a. Jesus always remains committed to us. He never denies us or leaves us.
    b. Jesus offered us the fullness of everything he had. He promised to be with us to the end of time.
    c. That's how we are to be with one another. Our focus is to be exclusively on our spouse. This means more than not committing adultery. It means that our mind and heart as well as our body belong only to our beloved.

2. *Jesus' love is forever.*
    a. His love is constant and unchanging.
    b. No matter how we behave, his love is unconditional.
    c. Unconditional love in marriage forces us to face our problems, including going to marriage enrichment and getting counseling in order to learn where we each need to change in order to build a deeper love.

3. *Jesus' love is intimate.*
    a. Jesus' love is so close, so intimate, that he has made us members of his body. We are literally part of him and he is part of us. He is aware of each of us.
    b. This does not mean that Jesus does not love everyone; he does. But he has a special love for those who choose to follow him.
    c. In the same way, we love all people—but we have a special love for one another that is profound in its intimacy—so powerful that even when we are not together, we carry each other in our hearts.

4. *Jesus' love is healing.*
    a. Jesus bragged about us to the Father in heaven.
    b. Jesus binds up all our wounds, spiritual, emotional or physical and cares for us himself.
    c. A great love relationship in marriage has the power to heal as we learn we are loved in all the stages of our lives, in all our moods and dispositions. Love reminds us we are lovable.

5. *Jesus' love is merciful.*
    a. Jesus tells us of the absolute importance of being mer-

ciful, i.e. forgiving the one who hurts us.   Forgiveness
is not an option for a Christian.

b. Again and again throughout the gospels, Jesus exhorts
us to forgive one another. As we forgive, we will be forgiven. As we judge, we will be judged.

c. Jesus' words often included the concepts of forgiveness
and healing. When he was dying on the cross he said,
"Father, forgive them; for they do not know what they
are doing" (Lk 23:34).

d. Each day of our lives we need to look at one another
with the eyes of mercy, not blaming, not criticizing--but
listening and caring with an open heart.

In order to look at how you and your beloved are
already bringing the love of Jesus to one another, complete
the following exercise.

* * * * *

A. What beautiful qualities does your spouse share in common with Jesus. How has your spouse made Jesus' love
alive for you? Go through the list below and put a checkmark next to all those qualities of love you have seen in
your spouse.

____   You have always stressed my good qualities. I always
feel affirmed by you.

____   You are not critical or judgmental of me.

____   You have always been faithful to me.

____   You have made me your first priority.

____   You brag about me to others.

____   You never threaten to leave me.

____   You are enthusiastic in your love for me.

____   You are willing to sit and talk with me—to share
your views and ideas and to listen to mine.

____   You are willing to work at deepening our relationship.

____   You are passionate in your love for me.

____   You are not afraid of intimacy.

____   You never hold a grudge or say "I told you so."

____   You are quick to forgive me when I have offended you.

____   You have never hit me, insulted me, or called me
names.

96

_____ You encourage me to try new things, take new risks because you are at my side.

_____ I always feel special when I'm around you.

_____ You are very tender and concerned when I don't feel well or I am upset about something.

Now go back through the list and put a * next to your spouse's strongest quality.

B. What qualities of Jesus' love do you plan to live out in your marriage? (Check all that apply.)

_____ I will love you with a passionate, life-giving, and holy love.

_____ I will be faithful to you not simply in sexual matters, but I will carry you in my mind and my heart wherever I go.

_____ I will make you my first priority—ahead of my friends and even my family.

_____ I will brag about your good qualities to others.

_____ I will not criticize you to friends.

_____ I will praise and affirm you so that you may grow in confidence and self-esteem.

_____ I will never threaten you with divorce even when I'm very angry with you.

_____ I will love you enthusiastically and show my love for you in all the big and little ways that make you happy.

_____ I will work on our relationship every day of my life.

_____ If our relationship becomes difficult, I will get counseling or look for help and encourage you to do the same.

_____ When I have hurt you, I will ask for your forgiveness.

_____ When you ask for forgiveness, I will always grant it to you.

_____ As far as I am concerned, this marriage is forever.

_____ I won't get into a pattern of blaming you when things go wrong.

_____ I will work on keeping our love alive and passionate, just as Jesus was passionate in his love for us.

Go back through the list and put a * next to the quality you feel most strongly about developing.

Now write a love letter to your spouse and include the following points:
1. Tell your spouse of the most beautiful quality you see in him/her. Give some examples of when you have experienced that quality.
2. Write of the quality you plan to develop more fully in your marriage. Be as specific as possible. Which quality will you develop? How will you do it? What changes are you willing to make in order to accomplish it? If you have time, you may write about more than one quality.
3. Close your love letter with words of love for your spouse.

When you have both finished writing, share your responses with each other.

Appendix:
When Should We Go for
Counseling?

It's hard to imagine that you'll ever need counseling when you are just beginning marriage and love for each other is strong. Many people still consider counseling to be a social stigma, and that acts as a barrier, preventing them from seeking help. Yet most people believe it's foolish to refuse to go to a medical doctor when there are physical symptoms indicating sickness. The disease will only get worse.

When we recited our vows and said "I do" in our Christian marriage, we made a commitment to each other and to the church to do whatever is necessary to keep our relationship healthy and growing. That means we committed ourselves to ask for help whenever our marriage appears to be troubled. In our parents' time (and that of their parents before them) many couples who knew their marriage was not healthy believed the right thing to do was to accept the suffering and go on living as husband and wife, even though it was a very painful and joyless relationship.

Today society is much more accepting of divorce. The result is that many Christian marriages are dissolved through divorce without the couples making a sincere effort to address their problems and ask for God's help in resolving them.

Where Do You Turn for Help?

Our society has become such a "rights-oriented" society that married couples who know things are going badly between them look immediately for a legal solution. The husband hastens to an attorney to learn what his rights are; the wife defends herself by getting her own attorney. In the typical case the attorneys get rich and the couple suffers even more. Because you are in a Christian marriage, the first place to turn for help is the church. Don't call the lawyer. Call the pastor. If you don't currently attend church, call a pastor from a nearby congregation.

The pastor has a special responsibility to offer you help. Some attorneys are altruistic, but basically you represent a financial interest to them. They also know from experience that once you come to them you have already decided your marriage is over and you are just asking them to help you end it in the best way possible relative to financial and child custody concerns.

The pastor is normally not a trained marriage counselor—though some are. The pastor is a trained spiritual counselor who can help you figure out how to renew your love for each other through the word of scripture and the wisdom of the church. In addition to seminary training, your pastor has years of experience in listening to many couples who have sought guidance. Do expect that he/she will listen attentively and nonjudgmentally to you. Don't expect that your pastor will offer you support for positions that go against church teaching.

It is important to know that your pastor will keep all of your sharing in confidence. Your pastor is also perceptive enough to know when you need to go to a professional counselor, and he/she can direct you to someone who is qualified professionally and is a Christian. Always turn first to the church for help in your marriage. As a first step, ask your pastor for some good books to read in the area of difficulty you are having in your marriage, or enroll in a marriage enrichment program.

When Should You Ask for Help?

If one partner thinks it's time to ask for help, no more evidence is needed. It's time to go to your pastor and seek guidance. If only one partner is willing to go at this time, ask your spouse to agree that he/she will go if the situation has not improved after a reasonable amount of time.

Some of the signs indicating it's time to seek help are:

1. If either partner is "acting-out" by abuse of alcohol or drugs, by an affair, by emotional abuse, by physical or verbal abuse, or by a domineering attitude.
2. Continual depression.
3. When there is continued unresolved conflict that is always surrounding the same issues.
4. Long periods of noncommunication with each other.
5. A poor sexual relationship, or none at all.
6. When you need an objective, third-party opinion.
7. When you find yourselves locked into a narrow point of view and you need outside input about new options you could try.

A Closing Prayer...

Loving God,
   Thank you for being with us today
   As we review our lives together,
   Our history and the events of our past
   As well as the experiences of the present.

   Today we consecrate our marriage to you.
   Help us to grow in the love you have given us.
   Help us to never lose sight of that love
   Or of you.

   We ask you this in the name of Jesus. Amen.

The Authors of DAY-BY-DAY

Dr. John J. and Kathleen A. Colligan live in Endwell, N.Y., and are the Directors of Family Life Education for the Roman Catholic Diocese of Syracuse, Southern Region.

They are also the Directors of the JOHN 17 CENTER, an international effort devoted to strengthening family life and renewing spirituality in local churches. They have presented hundreds of workshops throughout the U.S. and Canada on marriage preparation, marriage enrichment, Christian family spirituality, and inner healing. John and Kathleen have each received an M.A. in Adult Christian Community Development from Regis University in Denver, Colorado. They are the authors of *The Healing Power of Love* (Paulist Press, 1988) and *Evergreen* (Wm. C. Brown Publishing Co., 1989), a marriage enrichment program.